P9-DEW-259

DATE DUE

MAY 1 0 2002			
MAY 1 0 2002			
DEC 1 8 2009			
DEC 1 7 2009			
GAYLORD			PRINTED IN U.S.A.

DISCARDED

PANAMA.   12931
HASSIG, SUSAN.   972.87/HAS

SANTA FE HIGH SCHOOL LIBRARY

PANAMA

Susan Hassig

MARSHALL CAVENDISH
New York • London • Sydney

1

SANTA FE HIGH SCHOOL LIBRARY
SANTA FE, TX

Reference edition published 1996 by
Marshall Cavendish Corporation
99 White Plains Road
P.O. Box 2001
Tarrytown
New York 10591

© Times Editions Pte Ltd 1996

Originated and designed by
Times Books International, an imprint of
Times Editions Pte Ltd

All rights reserved. No part of this book may be reproduced or
utilized in any form or by any means electronic or mechanical,
including photocopying, recording, or by an information storage
and retrieval system, without permission from the copyright
owner.

Printed in Singapore

Library of Congress Cataloging-in-Publication Data:
Hassig, Susan M., 1969-
    Panama / Susan Hassig.
       p. cm.—(Cultures Of The World)
    Includes bibliographical references and index.
    ISBN 0-7614-0278-0 (lib. bdg.)
    1. Panama—Juvenile literature. I. Title. II. Series.
F1563.2.H38 1996
972.87—dc20   95–44491
                    CIP
                    AC

INTRODUCTION

PANAMA's geographic position has dominated its history and social, political, and economic life. As the narrowest isthmus between the world's largest oceans, Panama offers the world a 50-mile "bridge" that people once traversed on foot and now cross through the Panama Canal. The people of Panama reflect the cosmopolitan nature of their country. They originate from the many nations that have played a role in Panama's history. These include Spain, Africa, and the United States. A portion of Panama's population, the native tribes, occupied the country long before the Spanish arrived and still remain today.

Many people know about Panama only because of its canal and its dictatorial leaders. Yet Panama is a country of interesting people, rich traditions, beautiful topography, and magnificent native art. This book will tell you about Panamanians, their religious beliefs, customs, language, lifestyle, arts, and culinary delights. It will allow you to look beyond the canal and the dictators and learn much more about this remarkable country.

CONTENTS

Cuna women in their traditional attire, with nose rings, and beads around their wrists and ankles.

4

CONTENTS

Panama's national flower, The Flower of the Holy Spirit, blooms in August and September.

GEOGRAPHY

OVER 60 MILLION years ago, the floor of the Pacific Ocean began to divide and a ridge emerged out of the sea. This ridge developed over millions of years and became an isthmus that divided the Pacific and Atlantic oceans. Today, this isthmus is the country of Panama. Panama, meaning "an abundance of fish," is in the southern region of Central America, and its neighbors are Costa Rica to the west and Colombia to the east. The Pacific Ocean lies to the south and the Atlantic Ocean to the north.

Panama covers 29,762 square miles (77,084 square kilometers)—slightly smaller than the state of South Carolina. Only 216 miles (348 kilometers) of Panama are bordered by land, while the remaining 971 miles (1,562 kilometers) are coastline.

Panama's location and size make it the narrowest isthmus between the world's largest bodies of water, the Atlantic and Pacific oceans. From 1904 to 1914, over 75,000 laborers worked on a canal that would allow travelers to sail between the two largest oceans without having to go around South America. They built the Panama Canal across the narrowest point of the isthmus, which is only 50 miles (81 km) wide. Today, the Panama Canal is known as the gateway to the world.

Opposite: **The Gaillard Cut is the narrowest section of the Panama Canal.**

Below: **The lush rainforests contain many kinds of flora and fauna.**

TOPOGRAPHY

Although a relatively small country, Panama has a varied topography, including mountains, volcanos, jungles, rainforests, islands, magnificent white beaches, plains, and lowlands.

THE MOUNTAINS When Panama emerged from the sea, volcanic intrusions created mountain peaks. These mountains form a continental divide—to the east of the divide rivers flow to the Caribbean; on the western side, rivers flow to the Pacific Ocean.

Panama has several mountain ranges. The Serranía de Tabasará begins near the Costa Rican border and ends in a region of low hills in the middle of the country, near the Panama Canal. The Cordillera de San Blas and the Serranía del Darién lie east of the canal. Toward the Colombian border, these two ranges become part of the Andes, the great chain of mountains in South America.

THE RAINFORESTS Within several of the mountainous regions and along the Costa Rican and Colombian borders, Panama has dense rainforests. The Darién Gap, a region of rainforest and swamp, is located east of Colón and Panama City and extends to the Colombian border.

The rainforests are lush, green regions filled with trees, winding rivers, and wildlife. Scattered throughout the

The Serranía de Tabasará mountain range is the site of Panama's highest point, the Volcán Barú, which is 11,400 feet (3,475 m) high.

These mountains in central Panama are found near the market town of El Valle in Coclé Province.

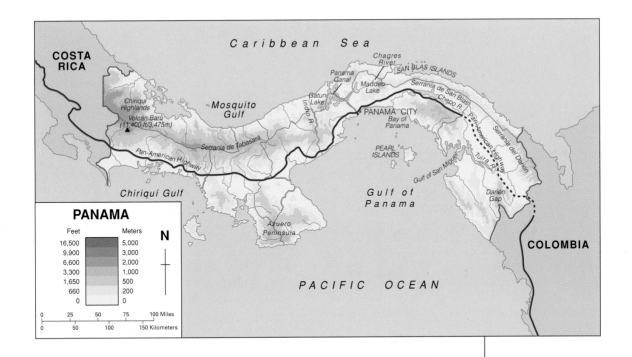

forests are small villages. As few Panamanians reside in the humid and dense rainforests, some areas of the forests are virtually unexplored by humankind.

THE ISLANDS Panama has thousands of small islands along the Caribbean and Pacific coasts. Beyond the white sands of the Caribbean coast are 365 small islands called the San Blas Islands. Palm trees dot the small islands, and coral reefs surround them. While many of the islands are uninhabited, the Cuna Indians live on several of the larger ones.

Along the Pacific coast of Panama are over a thousand small islands, including Contadora, one of the Pearl Islands, and Taboga, which has about 1,500 inhabitants. The waters surrounding the Pacific islands are famous for fishing and other water sports.

THE PLAINS Parts of central Panama are flatter and are called the "lowlands" or the plains. The majority of rural Panamanians live in the lowlands, and the towns of Penomoné, Chitré, and Las Tablas are in this region. The large province of Chiriquí is also located in the lowlands of central Panama; however, parts of Chiriquí are mountainous.

The lowlands have the longest dry season in Panama, but are still a productive area for agriculture.

9

The tropical rainforests, constituting almost 40% of Panama, are dwindling due to deforestation—the removal of trees.

As Panama lies in a tropical region, the humidity is high. The damp environment encourages the breeding of mosquitos.

CLIMATE

The climate of Panama varies little through the year. High temperatures along the coasts are between 85°F (30°C) and 90°F (33°C). The temperature on the Caribbean coast is slightly higher than the temperature on the Pacific coast. In the high mountainous regions, the climate often is markedly cooler. In the Darién region, however, the temperature is often very high, even hotter than in the coastal regions.

RAINFALL

The rainy season runs from May to December and the dry season from January to April. The average rainfall in Panama varies from less than 60 inches (152 centimeters) to almost 120 inches (305 centimeters) per year. Moisture from the oceans and forests is the primary contributor to the annual rainfall. The dense vegetation of the rainforests absorbs the water into its roots and pushes water vapors into the atmosphere through transpiration, which resembles sweating. These water vapors help replace

THE DARIÉN GAP

The Darién region of Panama, known as the Darién Gap, is the largest of Panama's regions and has the fewest inhabitants. The Darién Gap extends from east of Panama City and Colón to Colombia. Although this is the largest and one of the most beautiful regions in Panama, few Panamanians or tourists visit the Darién Gap because most of this area is accessible only by boat or canoe. For those who venture on foot into parts of the Darién Gap, a machete or other strong knife is needed to penetrate the dense jungle.

Historically, people have viewed the Darién Gap as a place of mystery and hidden wealth. Famous explorers such as Hernán Cortez, Vasco Núñez de Balboa, Christopher Columbus, and Francis Drake visited the area. Balboa was beheaded in this region in 1519, and Columbus supposedly had an attack of madness in the Darién Gap.

The Chocó and Cuna Indians of Panama reside in the dense Darién Gap. The largest concentrations of Chocós and Cunas live along the coasts or the Sambu and Sabalo rivers. The longest river in Panama, the Chagres River, runs through the Darién Gap and flows into the Caribbean Sea. The rivers of the Darién serve as highways, and often bathrooms, to the residents

of the area. The abundant flora and fauna of this region provide food for the Chocós and Cunas.

Humans are threatening to destroy the Darién Gap, one of the rare natural reserves in Central America. The Pan-American Highway, which begins in Fairbanks, Alaska, and ends on the southern tip of Chile, disappears for 67 miles (108 kilometers) in the Darién Gap. Despite protests from environmentalists and Indians, contractors claim that they will begin leveling this mysterious and brooding wilderness soon. Contractors, however, have been attempting to build the highway for years to no avail. The ongoing battle between those who seek to increase Panama's access to South America and those who strive to preserve the jungle will probably be resolved in the next decade as Panama gains complete independence from the United States in the year 2000.

the moisture in the air that falls as rain, making the air more humid and allowing rain clouds to form. As the trees are removed, the water drains from the cleared areas, and the roots of the remaining trees cannot absorb as much water. As a result, the amount of water available for evaporation decreases as does the annual rainfall.

Coral reefs off the San Blas Islands. As a result of a sharp rise in ocean temperatures over the past 15 years, some of the coral reefs in Panama's waters have died.

The Chocó Indians, who live in the rainforests, collect chunga and make it into beautiful masks, baskets, and bowls.

FLORA

Panama is host to 1,500 species of trees and 10,000 species of plants. The official national flower of Panama is the Flor del Espíritu Santo, or the Flower of the Holy Spirit. This flower is a beautiful white orchid that resembles a dove. One of the most interesting trees among the many species in Panama is the square tree. These trees, with trunks of an unusual square shape, are found in the mountains to the west of Panama City. Other flora found in Panama include small frangipani trees and heliconia plants.

In the tropical rainforests, banana, mango, guava, cocoa, and plantain grow in abundance. In addition there is a long, leafy grass called chunga, and growing along the many rivers are guilpa trees, which are giant, tangled trees with branches that form a canopy over the rivers. Snake-like vines grow on the guilpa trees, and surrounding the guilpas are other trees that contribute to the dense forest.

As a coastal country, Panama has a brilliantly colorful underwater world just offshore. In the Pacific Ocean plankton grows abundantly in the cold water. Along the Caribbean coast magnificent coral reefs thrive in the clear, warm waters.

FAUNA

Along with rich and varied flora, the small country of Panama is home to thousands of species of wildlife. For instance, Panama has over 900 species of birds, including parrots and toucans that live in the wild. One of the country's four national parks, the Soberanía National Park, holds the world record for the number of birds sighted within a 24-hour period—385 species of birds.

Less than a half-hour outside of Panama City, bands of howler monkeys swing through the trees. These, and other species of monkeys, also inhabit the rainforests of Panama. Sharing the rainforests with the monkeys are over 200 species of animals, including anteaters, pumas, jaguars, white-tailed deer, bats, iguanas, otters, opossums, crocodiles, and different types of rodents.

Several unusual types of wildlife are also found in Panama. These include tapirs and golden frogs. The frogs, creatures of mystery and intrigue, have skin that gleams the color of gold. This rare species is found in the mountains west of Panama City. Not much more than three inches in length, the golden frogs are said to travel miles to congregate in a single pond during mating season.

For centuries, the country of Panama has provided the nesting ground for thousands of migrating sea turtles. In the last decade, however, the number of turtles that visit Panama has dropped from 60,000 per year to 50,000 per year. Unfortunately, the decline in the number of turtles is due to a polluted environment and to people who have killed many of these beautiful sea creatures. Although the turtles provide a sense of immortality to the Panamanians, the people kill the turtles for their eggs, which are a delicacy, and their shells, which are taken to Asian countries to make jewelry.

In 1992, U.S. officials found five tapirs penned up at Manuel Noriega's estate and moved them to zoos for breeding. The discovery of these five tapirs will help ensure the survival of this endangered species.

13

SANTA FE HIGH SCHOOL LIBRARY
SANTA FE, TX

A rural family outside their home.

RURAL AND URBAN PANAMA

Approximately 45% of the population lives in rural Panama. The majority of rural Panamanians are either peasant farmers, ranchers, or teachers. Wealthy urban dwellers typically own large portions of rural land and hire peasant farmers to live on the land and cultivate it. By the late 1960s, many small farmers who owned their land sold it to the larger cattle ranches. Cattle ranches have rapidly expanded over the past few decades, absorbing rural land that previously was uninhabited.

PANAMA CITY The only Central American capital located on the Pacific Ocean is Panama City, the capital of Panama. Panama City, once called Castillo del Oro, or Castle of Gold, was founded in 1519. Today, almost one million people live in metropolitan Panama City.

PORTOBELO Along the Atlantic coast of Panama, in a sheltered bay, lies the beautiful village of Portobelo. Three forts now surround the city: San Andreas, San Felipe, and San Fernando. The Panama Canal Company removed a fourth fort in 1910 to use the stone in the locks of the Canal. Today, the village only has a few hundred inhabitants and the religious statue of the Black Christ, but its history makes it one of the most intriguing cities of Panama.

SANTA FE HIGH SCHOOL LIBRARY
SANTA FE, TX

Panama City's architecture ranges from old city ruins to contemporary glass and concrete buildings.

Recently, the Institute of Tourism of Panama approved a 10-year plan to develop visitor facilities such as beach resorts and casinos in hopes of increasing the number of international visitors to Panama City and the country itself. Under this plan, the government is hoping that investors will upgrade hotels and build new ones in Panama City.

The first European to discover this village was Christopher Columbus, when he took refuge in the bay in 1502. Within 100 years, Portobelo became a great trading center between Spain and its colonies in the New World. The gold and treasures of the Americas were shipped to the ports and loaded into galleons for Spain. Portobelo was attacked many times by English sailors and buccaneers, so Spain eventually decided to use a different port to ship its treasures, and Portobelo became less important.

Today, tin-roofed houses with black walls and no windows fill the small village. However, the village still holds its historical charm and reminds visitors of a time long-forgotten.

COLÓN At the Atlantic end of the Panama Canal lies the city of Colón, Panama's second largest city. Colón, like Panama City, is located within the Panama Canal Zone, an area under U.S. control until 1997.

Panamanians named Colón in honor of Christopher Columbus, while the U.S. citizens who were in Panama to build a railroad in the mid-1800s called the city Aspinwall. For many years, people referred to the city by both names. Eventually the Panamanian name of Colón became the official name after Panamanians refused to acknowledge and deliver mail to the city of Aspinwall.

HISTORY

WHEN THE SPANISH first arrived in Panama, they found three main groups of people. The Guaymí, related to the Maya of Mexico, lived near the modern Costa Rican border. The Chocó lived in western Panama. The Cuna resettled in the San Blas Islands to escape the Spanish. These peoples lived in circular, thatched houses and cultivated vegetables and fruit.

In 1501, Rodrigo de Bastidas became the first white man to set foot in Panama. One year later, Christopher Columbus established a trading post at Portobelo. Early explorers in search of gold and treasure almost destroyed the Panamanian natives by transmitted diseases, slavery, and the sword.

In 1510, Vasco Núñez de Balboa, a member of Bastidas' crew, settled in the Darién region. The settlers there elected Balboa and Martin Zamudio co-mayors of the first Panamanian city, Antigua. Balboa later set out in search of gold. He did not find gold, but on September 25, 1513, he became the first European to see the eastern shore of the Pacific Ocean, which he claimed for Spain.

When Balboa returned to Antigua in 1514, he found that the Spanish King Ferdinand had appointed a new governor named Pedro Arias Dávila, or Pedrarias the Cruel. In 1518, Dávila falsely charged Balboa with treason, arrested him, and had him beheaded.

Pedrarias the Cruel killed or enslaved thousands of Indians. A priest named Bartolomé de las Casas became outraged at the treatment of the Indians. At his suggestion, King Charles V of Spain exported over 4,000 African slaves to Panama to replace the Indian ones. This was the beginning of the slave trade to Central America, which lasted for more than 200 years.

Opposite: **In the old part of Panama City, only the tower remains among the ruins of the cathedral, which was attacked by pirates in the 16th century.**

Below: **Monument to Balboa in Panama City.**

THE SPANISH COLONY

From the 16th century until 1821, Spain retained control of Panama. In 1538, Spain established an *audiencia* ("ow-dee-EHN-see-ah"), or court, in Panama to administer Spanish territory from Nicaragua to Cape Horn. Because the area of this audiencia was so great, Spain established a new audiencia in 1563 to control the area that now constitutes the country of Panama.

TRADE MONOPOLY With Panama as one of its colonies, Spain retained a virtual monopoly on the trade of riches from other colonies near the Pacific Ocean. The other European countries challenged this monopoly and began to attack the Panamanian ports. Sir Francis Drake, an English buccaneer, attacked the ports, ambushed muletrains on the Royal Road, and looted the coastal cities from 1572 until 1596.

In 1597, Spain moved its Atlantic port to Portobelo. Sir Henry Morgan, another English buccaneer, held this port for ransom in 1668. He returned to Panama City in 1671 to loot it and eventually destroyed the city by fire. To halt the thousands of deaths and the destruction of cities, Spain signed a treaty with England in 1670 to defend the New World together. The peace did not last long, however, and Spain attacked and killed the English colonists who had survived disease and starvation in Panamanian settlements.

ENGLISH INTERVENTION Spain retained control over Panama, but England secured the right in 1713 to supply slaves to the Spanish colonies. Using this right, England smuggled trade goods aboard the slave ships, which weakened Spain's control over the isthmus. Spanish colonists who regarded Panama as their homeland and who wanted to be free of Spanish

Sir Francis Drake (1540–1596) was the first of many English buccaneers who attacked the Spanish colony of Panama in the 16th century.

Spain utilized the colony in Panama as a trade center and built a seven-foot-wide road across the colony, the Royal Road, to transport gold and silver from the Pacific Ocean to the Atlantic Ocean and then home to Spain.

18

The Spanish fort at Portobelo guarded Spanish treasure-carrying fleets from the pirates.

reign assisted the English in forming a contraband trade based in Jamaica. To combat its loss of control over Panamanians, Spain made the Panamanian audiencia a part of the Viceroyalty of New Granada, an audiencia that encompassed Colombia, Venezuela, and Ecuador.

In 1739, Spain and England went to war, and England destroyed Portobelo, which diverted Spanish trade from Panama. Without the transisthmian route through Portobelo, Spain lost much of its interest in the colony of Panama. The economy of Panama declined with the loss of its status as a trade center, primarily because the Panamanians neglected to develop another economic base before the loss.

INDEPENDENCE After the Spanish–English war of 1739, many of the Spanish colonies enlisted the help of England to separate from Spain.

Simón Bolívar eventually defeated Spain and liberated New Granada in 1819. The Spanish ruler fled Colombia and ruled in Panama until 1821. When the Spanish ruler died, another took his place for a short time and then left a Panamanian as the acting governor. On November 28, 1821, Panama declared its independence from Spain and became a part of Colombia.

After Panama declared independence, the country, together with Venezuela, Ecuador, and Colombia, was known as Gran Colombia.

COLOMBIAN CONTROL 1821–1903

Although Panama declared independence from Spain in 1821, Colombia controlled it from 1821 until 1903. Simón Bolívar assumed dictatorial responsibilities, and continued his attempt to unite the Spanish American republics, while others proposed a single vast monarchy.

A Venezuelan by birth, Simón Bolívar (1783–1830) played a significant role in freeing Panama from Spanish rule.

In his pursuit of complete independence from Spanish attacks, Bolívar requested protection from Britain. He invited Britain, as well as several other countries including the United States, to attend a conference in Panama in 1826. At this conference, Bolívar proposed a treaty that would bind Gran Colombia, Mexico, Central America, and Peru to defend each other and peacefully settle disputes. Colombia ratified the treaty, but it never became effective, and Bolívar died of tuberculosis in 1830 without seeing a united government.

Between 1830 and 1840, Panamanians attempted to break from Colombian control but were unsuccessful.

THE GOLD RUSH AND THE RAILROAD

In 1848, gold was discovered in California. Rather than traveling across the United States, prospectors sailed from the eastern United States to Panama, crossed to the Pacific on the Royal Road, and sailed on another ship to California.

On January 28, 1855, Panamanian workers completed a railroad across the isthmus. Approximately 6,000 workers died during the five years it took to build the railroad. The railroad earned over seven million dollars in its first six years, but the completion of a transcontinental railroad in the United States ended the golden years for the Panamanian railroad.

THE FRENCH CANAL During the 19th century, several countries, including the United States, Britain, and France, discussed building a canal across Panama or Nicaragua. The French engineer Ferdinand de Lesseps formed a canal company in 1879 to build a canal in Panama. He planned to build the canal within 12 to 18 years.

He officially began the project on January 1, 1880, but did not begin the work until 1881. By 1885, the workers had completed only 10% of the project and only about 20% of the workers were healthy enough to continue. De Lesseps' company went bankrupt in 1888 due to bad health among the workers and de Lesseps' refusal to build a canal that varied in level with the terrain. In 1889, work stopped on the canal, and thousands of workers, mostly blacks from the West Indies, were unemployed.

INDEPENDENCE FROM COLOMBIA In 1903, Panama proclaimed independence from Colombia with the assistance of the United States. A Panamanian named José Augustín Arango organized a revolutionary junta to overthrow the Colombian government. Arango knew that the United States wanted to construct a canal across Panama. In order to ensure that the commercial gains from the canal would go to Panama and not Colombia, he persuaded the United States to support Panamanian independence. On November 6, 1903, President Theodore Roosevelt recognized Arango's junta as the de facto government, and Panama became an independent protectorate of the United States.

Ferdinand de Lesseps built the Suez Canal but was unsuccessful in attempting a similar project in Panama.

Panama became a de facto protectorate, or dependent, of the United States whereby the United States guaranteed Panama's independence in return for control of Panama's domestic affairs.

21

THE PANAMA CANAL

For centuries, different countries had wanted to build a canal across Panama to link the world's largest oceans. In 1529, a Spanish priest drew the first plans for a canal, but Spain refused to build a canal that would help other nations. A famous explorer, Alexander von Humboldt, designed another plan for the canal in 1811, but lacked the technology to build his dream. From 1870 to 1875, the United States drafted seven possible routes for a Panamanian canal.

A few years after de Lesseps' project failed, the U.S. Senate ratified a treaty with Panama on February 23, 1904, which enabled the United States to build the canal. President Theodore Roosevelt appointed a commission to oversee the project. The commission hired John Findley Wallace, a 51-year-old civil engineer, to design the canal and William C. Gorgas, an Army doctor, to supervise all hospital and sanitary work.

BUILDING THE CANAL Unhappy with the intolerable working conditions and the commission's inability to progress on the canal, Wallace quit and President Roosevelt appointed John Stevens as the new engineer in 1905. Stevens began excavating in 1906 and soon discovered that he needed to build a lock canal, rather than a canal at sea level. However, he resigned in 1907.

During the first few years of canal building, Gorgas fought several battles to eliminate yellow fever and malaria, along with other deadly diseases that were killing the workers. Gorgas started a sanitation project that supplied running water to all the towns in the Canal

Construction work on the Panama Canal in progress in 1910. U.S. President Theodore Roosevelt signed a bill that authorized the United States to pay France $40 million for their land, equipment, buildings, and rights to the Panama Railroad.

Zone, established hospitals, destroyed the breeding grounds for disease-carrying mosquitos, and fumigated homes. By 1906, Gorgas had won the battle against yellow fever and malaria. He probably saved at least 71,000 lives and 40 million days of sickness.

After Stevens's resignation, Lieutenant Colonel George Goethels took over as chief engineer. He supervised the digging of the Culebra Cut, a channel through the mountains, at a cost of $14 million. The workers first built a dam to trap the water from the Chagres River into the lake created at Gatun. Then they built three double sets of locks, Gatun Locks, Pedro Miguel Locks, and Miraflores Locks, to raise the ships from sea level to the level of Gatun Lake—almost 85 feet (26 meters) above sea level—and back down to sea level again.

On August 15, 1914, the first ship, the Ancón, passed through the completed Panama Canal. After this maiden voyage, the Culebra Cut was renamed the Gaillard Cut, in honor of David Du Bose Gaillard who oversaw the blasting of the mountains. In 1966 the United States added channel lighting to allow ships to pass through 24 hours a day. The Bridge of the Americas, a mile-long highway, was built over the canal to connect Panama City with the west side of the canal.

Today, the Panama Canal is a living monument to the thousands of people who worked on it and to those who died to build a passageway between the Atlantic and Pacific oceans.

The Bridge of the Americas crosses the Panama Canal between the Miraflores Locks and the Pacific end of the Canal. This bridge links the Pan-American Highway between North and South America.

QUALIFIED INDEPENDENCE

Under the 1903 Hay-Bunau-Varilla Treaty, the newly independent country of Panama gave the United States the right to use, occupy, and control, in perpetuity, the land upon which it built the Panama Canal as well as sovereign rights within the Canal Zone.

Panama adopted a constitution in 1904 that was similar to the U.S. Constitution. In 1925, the Cuna Indians rebelled. The United States intervened in the revolt and convinced the Panamanian government and the Cunas to sign a treaty that recognized the San Blas Islands as a semiautonomous territory.

Panamanians, for the most part, resented U.S. involvement in their government and daily lives. After intervening several times in the 1910s and 1920s, President Franklin D. Roosevelt proposed, and Congress accepted in 1936, a principle of nonintervention in Panama. The two countries signed a treaty that same year that ended the protectorate and the United States' right to intervene. The treaty, however, did not alter U.S. sovereignty in the Canal Zone.

THE NEW REPUBLIC OF PANAMA

During World War II, the United States occupied 134 sites in the republic, including an airfield, a navy base, and several radar stations. In 1946, after the war, the United States wanted to keep the bases for another 20 years and Panama agreed. This agreement incited 10,000 Panamanians to revolt, resulting in the deaths of several students and police. As a result

The flags of two nations flying in the Canal Zone. By the early 1970s, some 40,000 U.S. citizens lived and worked in the Zone. Outside the fences, however, the Panamanians lived in poverty.

of the intense clash, the United States evacuated all its bases in Panama and outside of the Canal Zone and did not reoccupy them until 1955. The clash also was the first of several between angry students protesting the U.S. presence in their country and the Panamanian police. In 1958, a violent riot killed nine people. Another riot in 1959 prompted the United States to build a fence around the Canal Zone. In 1960, the United States agreed to fly the Panamanian flag in the Canal Zone, but several U.S. residents of the Zone refused to fly the flag. On January 9, 1964, almost 200 Panamanian students stormed into the Zone with their flag. After a struggle in which the flag was torn, thousands of Panamanians charged across the border fence and rioted. This three-day riot killed over 20 people and severely injured hundreds. The two nations eventually restored diplomatic relations.

A police officer in the Canal Zone, dressed almost identically to his U.S. counterpart.

After the series of riots and public dissatisfaction with the U.S. position in Panama, Panama requested new treaties, but the United States stalled the negotiations for a variety of internal reasons. Finally, under the leadership of President Jimmy Carter of the United States and General Omar Torrijos of Panama, the two countries signed a treaty on September 7, 1977, that gives Panama full control of the canal on December 31, 1999. They also signed another treaty, which provides that the canal remain neutral and open "to peaceful transit by all vessels of all nations on terms of entire equality." In war time, however, the United States and Panama, under the new treaty, have priority to the canal.

OMAR TORRIJOS'S RULE AND SUDDEN DEATH

On May 12, 1968, Panamanians reelected Arnulfo Arias as their president. Arias had served controversially in this role several times since 1940, and resumed his role as president on October 1, 1968. On October 11, the Panamanian military, the National Guard, removed Arias from his position after he attempted to remove two senior officers. The country fell into disarray for several months until Omar Torrijos Herrera and Boris Martínez of the National Guard assumed control.

Martínez's control was short-lived. After he provoked landowners and business persons they attempted to overthrow him in a coup. As a result, Omar Torrijos took full control and withstood several attempts to overthrow him.

Omar Torrijos was an effective leader. He was the son of schoolteachers and a friend of John Wayne, Fidel Castro, and British author Graham Greene. Torrijos referred to himself as a "populist," a governmental leader who represents and supports the common people. Torrijos reached out to rural Panamanians for political support, a group that had never been involved substantially in the government.

In 1970 the towns elected municipal council members who in turn confirmed Torrijos as Panama's head of government and approved a new constitution. As the head of government, Torrijos instituted wide changes in education, health care, public transportation, social programs, and foreign investment in the country. Most Panamanians adored Torrijos, but his opponents called him a tyrant because his improvements came at the cost of military rule. In 1978, Torrijos stepped down as head of government but remained head of the National Guard. Panama's national assembly appointed Aristides Royo as president.

On July 31, 1981, Torrijos's rule came to an abrupt end when his plane crashed in the mountains of western Panama. The cause of the crash has never been determined, but many people believed that General Manuel Noriega, who worked closely with Torrijos and later became commander-in-chief, planted a bomb aboard the small airplane. Since his death, Torrijos's supporters have paid tribute to him on the anniversary of his death and have turned his former residence into a history museum. Despite his reputation as a tyrant among his opponents, Omar Torrijos was one of the most important figures in Panamanian history, and his legacy and plans for the country continue today.

NORIEGA'S REIGN

After General Torrijos died in 1981, his chief of staff, Colonel Florencia Florez Aguilar, became the National Guard's commander-in-chief. Within a year, Aguilar retired and General Rubén Darío Paredes became the commander. On August 12, 1983, General Manuel Antonio Noriega Moreno (Manuel Noriega) became the commander-in-chief. Although Panama continued to elect a president, Noriega backed certain candidates and removed presidents who tried to usurp his power. Noriega continued to control the country until the United States invaded Panama on December 20, 1989, and forced Noriega to surrender and face drug trafficking charges in the United States.

Ernesto Perez Balladares, Panama's current president, is an experienced businessman with degrees from prestigious U.S. universities.

PRESIDENTIAL ELECTIONS

In May 1989 Panama held national elections. Foreign observers believe that Guillermo Endara, a fierce opponent of Manuel Noriega, won the election by a three-to-one margin. Despite the results Noriega voided the election and appointed Francisco Rodriquez the provisional president. After the United States intervened and ousted Noriega, Endara became president, Ricardo Arias Calderón became first vice-president, and Billy Ford became second vice-president.

In May 1994 Panama held its first election since the United States overthrew Noriega. Panama's popular salsa king, Rubén Blades, was a presidential candidate. Despite Blades' appeal in Panama, the country elected Ernesto Perez Balladares, who was a close friend and financial advisor of Torrijos. The people elected Tomas Gabriel Altamirano Duque first vice-president and Felipe Alejandro Virzi Lopez as second vice-president.

GOVERNMENT

PANAMA IS A CENTRALIZED republic that celebrates two independence days. Every November 3, Panamanians celebrate their independence from Colombia, and every November 28, they celebrate their independence from Spain. Beginning in the year 2000, Panamanians probably will celebrate another independence day on December 31. For on that date in 1999, the United States will hand over the canal to Panama, and leave the country.

Panama's Constitution, which was drafted in 1972 and amended in 1983, provides for a representative democracy with three separate branches of government: executive, legislative, and judicial. The people elect a president, two vice-presidents, and legislative representatives by secret ballot every five years. The executive branch appoints judges to 10-year terms.

Although the people elect the legislative and executive officials every five years, the 1968 coup d'état by the National Guard established an indirect military control of the government that lasted until 1990. The 1968 coup brought General Torrijos to power. He was succeeded by General Noriega. The National Guard became the Panama Defense Forces, or Fuerzas de Defensa de Panama (FDP), in the 1980s. The National Guard and FDP essentially controlled the government for over 20 years by handpicking presidential and legislative candidates and ensuring their victory through fraud or by removing the FDP opponent from office after the election. After Noriega's downfall, however, the FDP lost its de facto control of the government, and the constitution's democratic principles once again became the law.

Above: **The Presidential Palace is also known as Palace of the Herons, because live herons play in a large fountain located near the entrance of the residence.**

Opposite: **Workers staging a demonstration.**

MANUEL NORIEGA

In the slums of Panama City during the 1930s, a woman gave birth to a child who would grow to become the most notorious leader in Panama's history. This child, Manuel Noriega, grew up in the slums and left for a better life with the National Guard. When he was a cadet with the National Guard, he was arrested for beating and raping a prostitute. The Central Intelligence Agency of the United States convinced the Guard to keep Noriega and then paid Noriega to report on the Guard's communist tendencies.

While Noriega was serving as a police officer in Colón, Omar Torrijos found in him a young man whom he believed to be intelligent and loyal. When Torrijos assumed control of Panama in the late 1960s, he rewarded Noriega's loyalty to the Guard by appointing him the head of military intelligence. After Torrijos's death, there were two other men who briefly served as commanders-in-chief before Noriega became the head of the FDP in 1983.

As the head of the FDP, Noriega engaged in drug smuggling. Noriega continued to report to the CIA and the Drug Enforcement Agency, but only turned over the bare minimum of drug smugglers to avoid his own arrest. Noriega became personally wealthy by accepting money from Colombian drug dealers to allow them to pass cocaine shipments through Panama to the United States.

In 1987, opposition groups in Panama staged strikes and demonstrations against his regime, accusing him of drug trafficking, election fraud, and the murder of political rivals.

In 1988, two Florida grand juries indicted him on drug trafficking charges. Noriega ignored the charges and continued to run the country until late 1989. U.S. President George Bush ordered 24,000 troops into Panama on December 20, 1989, to capture Noriega. Noriega, who had declared that Panama was in a "state of war" with the United States five days before the invasion, went into hiding and encouraged Panamanians to "win or die." During a two-week search for Noriega, 300 Panamanian soldiers, hundreds of civilians, and 12 U.S. soldiers died. The general found asylum in the Vatican Embassy in Panama on December 24. The United States miltary forces played loud rock music outside the embassy until Noriega surrendered on January 3, 1990. A jury in Florida convicted Noriega of drug trafficking, and he currently resides in a Miami jail cell.

PANAMA'S CONSTITUTION

Panama first adopted a constitution in 1904 that was similar to the U.S. Constitution. In 1976, Panama adopted the constitution that remains law today, with a few amendments in subsequent years. One recent amendment to the constitution abolishes the armed forces. Because the military had always played a dominant role in Panama's politics, this amendment drastically changed the law.

The constitution provides personal rights to Panama's citizens. These personal rights include the freedom of speech and press, the right to form political parties and other professional or civic groups without government interference, freedom of religion, freedom to move within the country and to leave and return to the country, and the right to have an attorney represent a citizen charged with a crime. Panama's Constitution establishes the procedures for electing and appointing government officials.

Courthouse, Panama City. In Panama, the judiciary is made up of a nine-member Supreme Court of Justice, five superior district tribunals, 27 circuit judges, and 84 municipal judges.

PANAMANIAN LAWS

Panama also has many laws, including civil, criminal, and labor codes. After years of tyranny by the National Guard and FDP, the government, through new laws and codes, is stressing human rights in the home, workplace, and prison. The government continues to investigate political murders that occurred during the military dictatorship and is trying defendants accused of murdering, kidnapping, and torturing individuals during this period.

A political rally in Panama City.

POLITICAL PARTIES

Since the 1994 elections, Panama has had eight official political parties: the Democratic Revolutionary Party (PRD), the Arnulfista Party (PA), Papa Egoro (Mother Earth), Molirena, the Christian Democrats, Morena, Renovación Civilista, and Partido Solidaridad. To retain its status as an official political party, a group must attract at least 5% of the national vote for its candidates.

President Balladares is a member of the left-center PRD party. His party previously supported Manuel Noriega, but Balladares has vowed to distance himself from Noriega and heal the wounds of Panama's past. Balladares offered cabinet posts to members of other political parties such as the PA, the Partido Solidaridad, and the Christian Democrats.

The political parties of Panama have different views on the role of government in a society. For instance, the PA is a party that opposes communism and supports nationalism, while the PRD believes in nationalist and social policies. Another major party, the Christian Democrats, supports private enterprise and social reforms.

Panama's Constitution prohibits discrimination against individuals based on race, illegitimacy, social class, sex, religion, or political views.

THE CUNAS' SELF-GOVERNMENT

In 1925, the Cuna Indians rebelled against the government and declared themselves an independent state. Today, they are politically autonomous.

The Cunas' political life centers around a nightly "gathering" of the community. During a gathering, the Cuna men, who make up a congress, meet with the chiefs and discuss business, delegate duties, and recall religious and historical traditions. Medicine men also attend the gatherings to use herbs, chants, and idols to heal illnesses among the tribe.

The Cunas also discuss and resolve any disputes among tribe members at the gathering through mutual consensus. According to Cuna law, an individual who commits a wrong against another member of the tribe must speak before the tribe at the gathering. Otherwise, the tribe will not rejudge, replay, or recall the wrong.

Several times each year, every village sends at least one chief and another member of the village tribe to a general congress. The general congress holds a gathering similar to the ones in the individual villages where they exchange information and resolve matters or disputes.

The Cunas hold two types of gatherings: the chanting gatherings that all of the Cunas attend and the speaking gatherings that only the men attend.

ECONOMY

PANAMA'S KEY LOCATION as a port historically has bolstered its economy. Beginning in the early 1500s, settlers and sailors used the isthmus to transport goods from the Pacific Ocean to the Atlantic Ocean. The port cities prospered from Spain's colonial trade and became dependent on world commerce for their prosperity. The flow of goods also discouraged Panamanians from producing their own products.

Opposite: **A worker tends a gladiolus field in the rich soil of the Chiriquí highlands.**

Until the late 20th century, Panama's economy fluctuated with international trade cycles. After Spain stopped using Panama's port to transport goods due to raids by pirates in the 1700s, the economy declined and the country was barely self-supporting. When gold was discovered in California in the 1800s, Panama's economy boomed when thousands of goldrushers sailed into its Atlantic ports and traveled across the country via foot or railway.

When the United States built a transcontinental railroad, Panama's economy again declined. In the 1800s and early 1900s, the economy surged as France began and the United States completed a canal across the isthmus. During the worldwide depression in the 1930s, the economy fell.

Above: **This train runs between Panama City and Colón. When the Panama Canal was completed, there was a surge in the economy of these two cities at either end of the canal.**

World War II, however, provided a necessary stimulus to Panama's economy when U.S. forces moved onto the isthmus. After the war, the economy continued to expand due to the canal, agricultural output, banana exports, and a sophisticated commercial and retail system. In the past 20 years, Panama's economy has fluctuated. Today, it is on the rise, but over 50% of the citizens continue to live in poverty.

Panamanian secrecy laws for banks are similar to those in Switzerland. Thus, foreign investors often deposit funds in these banks that they wish to keep secret from someone or some agency, such as the Internal Revenue Service.

THE BALBOA

The balboa, named after the great explorer and Panamanian leader, circulates only in coin. The U.S. dollar is the paper currency. One balboa is equal to one dollar, and 100 centesimos constitute one balboa.

PANAMA'S FINANCIAL SYSTEM

CURRENCY The official currency in Panama is the U.S. dollar, and the local currency is the balboa. As the official currency, the dollar is the principal means of exchange, which attracts foreign capital that uses the dollar as currency. The dollar also has contributed to Panama's low inflation rate, the lowest on the continent. Another contributor to Panama's stable environment is the freedom to move funds in and out of the country without charge.

TAX SYSTEM Panama has a territorial tax system, that is, it only taxes profits earned within the country. For instance, if a Panamanian company makes a profit through international trade, the profit is tax-exempt. This

Panamanian currency—the balboa.

tax-exempt status on international profits encourages the growth within Panama of international and commercial banking activities. Furthermore the government will not tax the interest on deposits and bonds registered at the local exchange rates. This policy encourages corporations and individuals to deposit profits in Panamanian banks.

BANKING Over the past two decades, Panama has emerged as an important international banking center. Over 100 local and foreign banks constitute Panama's banking center, and over 200 branches are located in Panama City and in other principal population centers. In the past few years, the total assets and deposits of the banks have exceeded 20 billion dollars each.

Panama became an international banking center during the Torrijos years. Banks from foreign countries were attracted to Panama's dollar-based economy, its historical status as a trade center, and its policy of low taxes on deposits and income. In addition, the banks' customers were attracted to secrecy laws that prohibited the banks from disclosing information about their customers.

Within Panama are over 50 banks with general licenses that permit the banks to offer a wide range of services within the country and internationally. Almost 30 of Panama's banks have international banking licenses that permit them to negotiate international banking transactions from a local office. Also located in Panama are banks with representative licenses, or banks that establish an office solely to represent another entity. According to Panamanian law, a bank must fit within one of these three categories to qualify for a license.

THE GROWTH OF THE STOCK MARKET In the past decade, Panama has established a stock market, which has increased Panama's role as an international financial center. Prior to 1990, no formal stock exchange existed; but in 1990, La Bolsa de Valores de Panama started operating as the only Panamanian exchange. The market is growing, and Panama is becoming an ideal location for regional exchange due to its location, bilingualism, dollar-based economy, and the territorial tax system. Additionally, Panama's newest president has expressed a strong interest in supporting the local stock market, as well as other international economic policies.

The high confidentiality of Panama's banks have contributed to the rise of the banking sector.

EMPLOYMENT

One of the largest employers in Panama since the beginning of the 20th century has been the Panama Canal. In the early days the canal employed builders and engineers. Today, it employs thousands of Panamanians and U.S. citizens working for the canal itself or in the Zone.

A large majority of Panamanians work in the urban areas as professionals in business, medicine, banking, and law. Urban Panamanians also work in retail, the restaurant business, and museums. In addition to service areas of employment, many Panamanians work in agriculture, industry, and the public sector.

Panamanian citizens who are able to work are either employed, unemployed, or "informally employed." The city streets are lined with the latter type of employee. These people, who often used to be professionals, now work as street vendors and peddlers by selling handicrafts, market items, and other inexpensive goods on the sidewalks.

This woman selling lottery tickets is one of some 14% of the employed persons in Panama who work "informally" as street vendors.

During the 1990s Panama became one of the top five leading countries in Latin America to increase wages and reduce unemployment. Despite the progress compared to other nations, however, almost 50% of Panamanians continue to live in poverty. The Planning and Economic Policy Ministry of Panama has estimated that over 40% of Panamanian families earn less than 100 balboas per month, while the food for this same family for one month costs over 200 balboas. The ministry also estimates that over 15% of the population that is able to work is unemployed.

PROFITS FROM LAND AND SEA

Before the United States constructed the canal, most Panamanians worked on the land. Even in the 1950s, the agricultural sector contributed almost 30% of the country's Gross Domestic Product (GDP). In 1994, agriculture, forestry, and fishing combined only contributed 10.8% to the GDP. Over 26% of Panama's people worked in the fields of agriculture, forestry, and fishing in 1994. Chief agricultural products are sugar cane, rice, corn, coffee, beans, tobacco, chicken, cattle, milk, eggs, and fish.

Panama's chief exports are bananas, shrimp, coffee, raw sugar, and petroleum products. Bananas are the leading export, with annual profits of approximately $220 million. The United States owns Panama's largest banana plantation, which is in the province of Chiriquí and accounts for around 70% of Panama's banana production. Chiriquí is also the site of most of Panama's coffee plantations. Panama exports coffee to the United States, Canada, Saudi Arabia, Germany, Italy, and nine other European countries.

FISHING The fishing industry provides both the domestic and international markets with a variety of fish from the Atlantic and Pacific oceans. Many kinds of fish as well as lobster and shrimp are found in Panama's coastal waters. Shrimp is the most profitable and largest fishing product, followed by anchovies and herring. Most of the shrimp farms are located near Aguadulce on the Pacific coast. The industry processes the anchovies and herring into food, fish meal, and oil.

The coffee industry has suffered from falling prices over the past few years, and exported 37% less coffee in 1994 than it did in 1993.

The government passed a labor code in 1972 that expanded employment opportunities and improved Panama's international status in agriculture and industry. The labor code also gave employees more security, benefits, and bargaining power with the employer.

AGRARIAN REFORM IN THE 1970S

Panamanian land before the 1950s was available to anyone who wanted to clear and cultivate it. As deforestation increased, so did the population as people moved onto the cleared land. Because less land became available for farming, the settlers often planted crops too soon after clearing the land. This caused a decrease in the crops and an increase in unemployed farmers who could not make enough money to stay on the rural land.

When Omar Torrijos took over Panama, one of his goals was to decrease poverty and increase employment. Torrijos believed that land, or agrarian, reform would help him meet his goal. Between 1969 and 1977, the government redistributed land and organized farmers into collective agricultural groups. To redistribute land, a government commission acquired 1,235,000 acres (500,175 hectares) of land and gave individual and collective lots to over 18,000 families.

In addition to redistributing land, the commission borrowed a Chilean system that organized farmers into collective agricultural groups. Under this system the government extended assistance to the peasants within the groups by providing them with credit, training, new roads, wells, and health programs. The government also encouraged the groups to pool land and collectively farm the land.

The agrarian reform cost the government a tremendous amount of money, but the incomes of the cooperative farmers remained low. By the late 1970s, the government stressed productivity rather than equity among the farmers. Although the reform did not produce the economic results that the government desired, the peasant farmers benefited from the reform in many ways: health programs reduced the mortality rate, and the wells increased the farmers' access to safe water. Additionally, training and school programs enabled rural Panamanians to become more educated.

MANUFACTURING

Panama's industries produce cigarettes, alcoholic and carbonated beverages, processed sugar, salt, fish meal and fish oil, and paper products. The manufacturing sector contributed almost 8% of the GDP in 1994. Over 60% of the manufacturing plants are located in Panama City; smaller industrial centers are in David and Colón.

Tourists buying molas from Cuna Indians. Panama's extensive transportation system has helped make it a popular spot for tourists. The profits from tourism inject millions of dollars into the Panamanian economy.

TRANSPORTATION

Throughout its history, Panama has focused on its transportation system. The Spanish built the Royal Road in the 16th century to transport goods across the isthmus. A few centuries later Panama built its railroad across the isthmus to link the two oceans. Finally, in the early 20th century, the United States built the canal.

Panama also has a network of highways and roads that link its cities to each other and to other countries. The Pan-American Highway, which stretches from Alaska to Chile, runs through Panama, interrupted briefly in the Darién Gap. The Trans-Isthmian or Boyd-Roosevelt Highway links Panama's major cities, Panama City and Colón. Today Panama has three railroads: two in the west and one linking Panama City and Colón.

Panama also has an extensive international transportation system. Although the country is only as large as South Carolina, it has 14 ports and eight airports. The ports are scattered along the coasts: the two most important are Balboa and Cristóbal. The airports are located in Panama City (both the Paitilla Airport and the Tocumen), Bocas del Toro, Changuinola, Contadora, Colón, David, and San Miguel.

The oil pipeline that runs between terminals owned by Panama and the United States is another important transportation system in Panama.

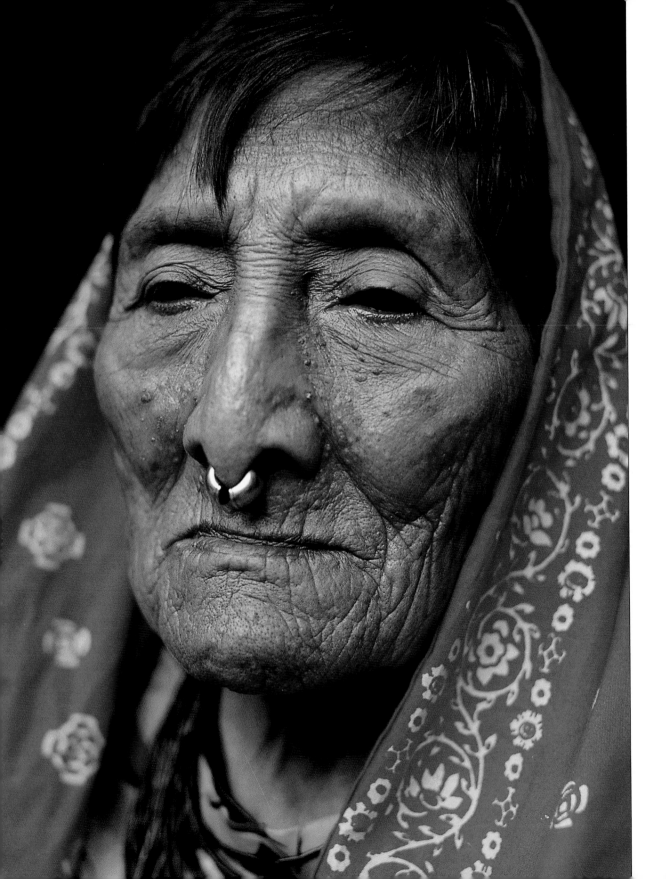

PANAMANIANS

THE PEOPLE OF PANAMA are primarily a mix of several different ethnic groups. Panamanian *mestizos* ("may-STEE-zos") are a mingling of indigenous Indian groups with descendants of Spanish settlers. Approximately 60 to 70% of the 2.54 million people in Panama are mestizos. Another 14% of Panamanians are Afro-Caribbean, 6% are Indians, and the remaining 10 to 20% are immigrants from North America, Asia, France, Italy, and Greece. This last group primarily consists of the social elite.

Opposite: Traditional Cuna woman. Cuna women begin wearing nose rings when they are infants.

Ethnicity is an important social distinction in Panama, yet the Panamanian subcultures have merged to the point that individuals are often difficult to classify as belonging to a particular ethnic group. Thus, ethnic groups in Panama are not as segregated as ethnic groups in the United States. Nonetheless, Panamanians classify themselves into three principal groups: the Spanish-speaking Roman Catholic mestizos; the English-speaking Protestant Afro-Caribbeans; and tribal Indians.

Above: Panamanian youths relaxing in a public square.

The mestizos and Afro-Caribbeans reside in both the cities and the rural areas. The majority of tribal Indians live in the more remote regions such as the San Blas Islands and the Darién region. The Panamanians of foreign descent, including the whites, primarily reside in the larger cities.

The origin of the Cunas is somewhat of a mystery. Cunas themselves do not agree on their origin: some Cunas claim to be of Carib descent, while others believe that the god Olokkuppilele in Colombia created them.

The Cunas are extremely short and have brown skin. If a Cuna is 5'2" (1.58 meters) tall, he or she is considered very tall.

TRIBAL INDIANS

Historians say approximately 500,000 to 800,000 Indians from over 60 tribes lived in Panama before the Europeans arrived in the 16th century. The three largest groups of Indians at that time were the Cuna, the Chocó, and the Guaymí. These tribes remain today.

The Cunas have been linked to the Andean, Arawak, Carib, Chibcha, Cueva, and Coiba tribes. The Guaymís are related to the Mexican and Central American Nahuatlan and Mayan nations. The Chocós are related to the Chibcha tribe of Colombia.

When the Spaniards arrived they conquered the tribes and enslaved, tortured, and killed the Indians. Many of the Indians who survived the brutality died of European diseases. A priest, Bartolomé de las Casas, saved the Indians from their oppressors when he suggested that the Spaniards replace the Indian slaves with Africans. Although this decision made slaves of another race, it allowed the Indians to escape the Spaniards and move into the remote areas of Panama where they still live.

Today, the Cuna, Chocó, and Guaymí peoples, along with a few smaller tribes, constitute approximately 6% of the population. Many of the Indians are assimilating into the general population, while others remain in the more remote regions. The smaller tribes of Panama are the Bribri, which live near Costa Rica, the Bókata in eastern Bocas del Toro, and the Térraba, in the northwest corner of Panama. The tribes are under the jurisdiction of the national and provincial governments, but many tribes remain virtually autonomous.

The Guaymís, who make up more than half of the Indian population, live in the northwest regions in hamlets. The hamlets house related men, their wives, and their unmarried children. Often grandparents, parents, and married children live in the hamlet as well. The hamlet defines a person's social identity, and individual roles within the hamlet are well-defined. The Guaymí tribe functions as a group and makes decisions that are informal and consensual.

A Guaymí family in Bocas del Toro Province.

Most of the Cuna Indians live on 52 of the San Blas Islands and along the Darién coast. Although the Cunas were the largest tribe before the Spaniards arrived, today the tribe constitutes about one-third of the Indian population. The Cunas, more than any other tribe, have retained their cultural heritage and racial purity. The Cunas produce the world's greatest percentage of albinos.

SOCIAL SYSTEM

Panama's social system has three main tiers: the elite, the middle class, and the lower class. The class structure divides citizens based on wealth, occupation, education, family background, culture, and race.

THE ELITE The Panamanian elite generally live in the cities. The elite class consists of a group of wealthy, old families of Spanish descent and immigrants, such as North Americans, who became wealthy through commerce or the Canal. While the elite status is usually earned through birth and breeding, some Panamanians have entered this class through education. Panamanians view a profession, such as law or medicine, as a status symbol and a gateway into the political arena. Most elite families send their children to Western Europe or the United States for college and graduate work. The elite families strongly encourage their children to marry within their class.

A middle-class family on an outing. Middle-class parents typically encourage their children to become professionals, government officials, or teachers.

THE MIDDLE CLASS Like the elite, most members of the middle class reside in the cities; however, some small towns have middle-class residents. Mestizos predominate in the middle class, yet some Afro-Caribbeans have moved into this class; so have descendants of the railroad workers and immigrants from other countries. The members of this class continually strive, through education and emulation of elite behavior, to elevate their status.

One person's refuse is another's gold. Two young boys rummage through trash cans outside the U.S. Canal Zone.

THE LOWER CLASS Most rural Panamanians belong to the lower class. In the countryside, people struggle to survive poverty and many leave the countryside for a better life in the cities. These migrants find work in the cities as semi-skilled laborers and servants. Despite their efforts, some of these Panamanians have not managed to attain a higher social status. Over the past few decades, however, some ethnic groups have become more educated and wealthy, and thus have moved up the social ladder. The Afro-Caribbeans, for example, have moved from their status as laborers to middle- and upper-class positions in Panamanian society. Education has been the key to their advancement in the social hierarchy.

THE ORIGINS OF THE PANAMANIAN SOCIAL SYSTEM

Panama's social system began in Spanish colonial times and has continued until today. The Spanish miltary and colonists exploited the Indians, conquering their lands, shipping treasure back to Spain, and enslaving and killing them. They brought African slaves to the Caribbean. The Indians and Africans made up the lower levels of society. The middle class emerged when people moved out of the settlement areas and formed smaller societies. This class usually did not use slaves, and because they did their own work, the elite class looked down on them.

Panamanian folk dancers
resplendent in their traditional attire.

CLOTHING

Panamanians are fairly conservative and formal in their dress. Within the city businessmen often dress less formally than those in the United States. For instance, men often wear a cotton shirt called a *guayabera* ("gay-ah-BAY-rah"), which is a loose-fitting, short-sleeved cotton shirt that is not tucked into the trousers. In some professions, such as banking and law, men and women wear lightweight suits.

Panamanians frown on wearing shorts in public, no matter how hot it is. Men may occasionally wear shorts, but society considers it inappropriate for women to wear shorts or trousers in public. Although Panamanians grant leniency to tourists who wear shorts in the city and countryside, they prefer that foreigners abide by their somewhat stringent dress code.

TRADITIONAL CLOTHING FOR WOMEN The national dress for women is the *pollera* ("poh-YEH-rah"), which is a long, full dress of white cotton. Brightly colored embroidery adorns the beautiful dress, and the women wear it for national celebrations, carnivals, and special occasions. The *peineta* ("peh-ee-NEH-tah") is the headpiece that the women wear with the pollera. The peineta consists of veils or elaborate, large combs with dangling ornaments.

Cuna women also have a traditional dress that consists of a blue print wrap-around skirt similar to that worn by the ancient Egyptians, a gold ring in both the nose and ears, strings of yellow and red beads around the arms and legs, a black line on the nose, and a blouse with *mola* ("MOH-lah") panels. A mola is an intricate and brilliantly colored design on a panel of cloth. Typically, a blouse will have one mola on the front and another on the back. Cuna women's attire varies based on their marital status, and an unmarried woman wears her hair long, while a married woman cuts hers short.

TRADITIONAL CLOTHING FOR MEN The traditional clothing for men in Panama is the *montuno* ("mohn-TOO-noh"). The montuno is a white cotton embroidered shirt and short trousers. As part of this traditional garb, men often wear a straw hat called a *pintado* ("pin-TAH-doh"). This hat has a distinctive curled-up brim and black patches on it. With this outfit, men wear sandals.

The pollera de gala *("poh-YEH-rah de GAH-lah") is the "deluxe" pollera and consists of several intricately embroidered petticoats under a full, embroidered skirt. The petticoats and the skirt are made of fine material and lace, and the embroidery, called* aderozo *("ah-deh-ROH-soh"), is colorful. The blouse of the pollera de gala also has intricate embroidery designs, and a woman wears the blouse off the shoulders.*

LIFESTYLE

LIFESTYLE IN PANAMA varies according to region and ethnicity. One thing all Panamanian families have in common, however, is the importance of the family. Panamanians consider their family to be their support, their responsibility, and the ultimate recipient of their loyalty. Along with loyalty to family members, Panamanians value their friendships and interact with their friends as friends do in the United States.

Panamanians are an eclectic group of immigrants from many countries, and they readily accept other groups' cultures and combine them with their own. The Panamanian lifestyle shows Caribbean rather than South American influence. The Caribbean influence is unusual because Colombia controlled Panama for many years.

Social gatherings in Panama have certain customs that guests follow. For instance, guests at large social gatherings introduce themselves to other guests and do not expect the host or hostess to introduce them. Guests at these large parties do not arrive on time. Even if the party begins at 10:00 p.m., Panamanians consider arriving two hours late to be acceptable. At a smaller party, however, a guest should not arrive later than a half-hour after the starting time. For all parties, a Panamanian host or hostess appreciates a small gift from each guest.

Opposite: **A Cuna settlement. The Cunas live in thatched palm huts with bamboo walls.**

Above: **A Panamanian family outside their home in Colón Province.**

51

FAMILY LIFE

Panamanians are very loyal to their family and have historically viewed their family ties as a defense against an uncertain and hostile world. Often, Panamanians are more loyal to their parents and siblings than to their spouses. In many Panamanian families, particularly those in rural areas, three generations live under one roof. Family members steadfastly come to each other's aid, if needed, and support each other throughout life.

A Cuna family outside their home. Cuna Indians' close family ties and their remote location have enabled them to preserve a distinct ethnic identity.

FAMILY LIFE FOR THE CUNA INDIANS
The Cunas live on the San Blas Islands or in the Darién region.

The family is important to the Cuna Indians, and many members of one family will live in a single hut. Men dominate Cuna society and the family, and the most senior man in a hut is the head of the household. When a daughter marries, her husband comes to live with her family, and the husband is subordinate to the father. The husband often tries to establish his own household after a few years.

The women perform the household duties and sew for the family. In their spare time, they make molas, often at night with the help of a kerosene lamp. The women inherit the land that they live on from their fathers. Thus, parents hope for female children.

FAMILY LIFE FOR THE GUAYMÍ INDIANS Guaymí Indians live with their family in a hamlet. The hamlets are scattered throughout the Guaymí region but do not form villages or towns. A Guaymí couple will either live with the husband's family or the wife's family.

The Guaymís have defined roles for men and women. For instance, the women do not clear the forest, hunt, or herd cattle, but they chop firewood. The men usually do not care for the children, cook, or clean. The children begin to help their parents with the chores when they are 8 years old, and their parents expect them to do the work of an adult by the time they are 14 if a girl, or 17 if a boy.

FAMILY LIFE FOR THE CHOCÓ INDIANS A much smaller tribe than the Cunas or Guaymís, the Chocós live deep within the Darién jungle in small groups of one or two extended families. Over the past few decades, the Panamanian government has encouraged the Chocó Indians to congregate and attend schools within villages.

A Chocó family lives in a bamboo hut on stilts with a cone-shaped roof. The Chocós climb a ladder to their home, then pull it up after them so that animals cannot climb into the hut.

MARRIAGE

The majority of Panamanian men and women choose their own spouses. Couples, particularly rural middle-class and lower-class ones, often decide to marry and have children together, but do not participate in a formal marriage ceremony until years later. Although the children of these "marriages" are born out of wedlock, they bear no stigma. These children often encourage their parents' formal marriage. If the unions between these unmarried couples do not work out, the woman usually keeps the children.

Many Panamanians, particularly the elite and middle classes, choose to participate in a formal marriage ceremony before starting a life with another person. Among these classes, marriage plays an integral role in maintaining or improving a family's social status. Although the families do not arrange the marriages, they encourage their children to marry individuals of wealth and racial purity.

Marriage plays an integral role among the native tribes in Panama. The Cuna Indians do not marry outside the tribe in order to maintain their racial purity. The Guaymí Indians view marriage as the most important event in a person's life. Fathers usually arrange their children's marriages based on the selected spouse's access to land and wealth and position in the tribe. Some Guaymí men practice polygamy, or marriage to more than one woman. An older man often marries his wife's younger sister, and the wives raise their children together.

A Panamanian bride poses for the camera on her wedding day.

CHOOSING GODPARENTS

To Panamanians, godparents symbolize trust and loyalty. Children's relationships with their godparents are significant both religiously and morally. Thus parents choose godparents whom they trust and respect. The godparents, in turn, provide guidance, love, and assistance to the godchild.

Panamanians differ on whether godparents should be of higher economic and social status than the parents. Some Panamanians choose godparents from a higher social status to assist the child in gaining influence and power. Other Panamanians, however, believe that the choice of a godparent should reflect existing social ties and should not be an attempt to elevate social status.

BIRTH

Most Panamanians desire children and celebrate their birth. As in the United States, some people opt not to marry or have children, but the overwhelming majority of Panamanians hope for children.

When a couple has a child, they take great care in choosing godparents for the child. Most Panamanians believe that the godparents play an integral role in the child's life; thus, the selection process is an important one for the couple.

The Cuna Indians have large families, and a couple hopes for a girl so that when she marries, she will bring a son-in-law into the family. For the first month of an infant's life, the mother breastfeeds the child. After one month, the infant drinks a banana drink. When the infant is 10 months old, he or she begins to eat solid food.

Life for Panamanian infants is difficult. For every 1,000 infants born each year, approximately 21 die at birth. This death rate is high, especially considering the Panamanian government's emphasis on improving health care. Over 25% of Panama's infants suffer from malnutrition; and infants in the rural areas suffer 3.2 times more than those in the cities. Unfortunately, even though parents desire the birth of a child, they often are too poor to provide adequate food for their children.

The average size of a Panamanian family is 4.4 persons, and in over 22% of these families a woman is head of household.

A communal work group clearing forest in the mainland.

MEN AND WOMEN

Over the past few decades the roles of Panamanian men and women have changed. Although most women still do not enjoy the same economic, social, and educational opportunities as men, women's opportunities have improved. Today, more women are attending secondary and upper level schooling. Women are also entering fields that were traditionally male-dominated in the past, such as medicine, banking, and law.

In the past (and continuing to a degree today) Panamanian men and women had clearly defined roles in society. Parents sent their sons to better schools and gave them more freedom than their daughters. Men dominated not only the workplace, but the home as well. Society allowed and expected married men to have mistresses and support the children that the mistresses bore them. Married women, on the other hand, were required to be faithful to their husbands.

In rural society, men and women have traditional sex roles. The men work outside of the home farming and raising crops or animals, while the women stay at home and care for the children. Many rural women are illiterate, because female education is a low priority for peasant families.

Men and Women

The native tribes of Panama have similar societal roles for men and women. The men and women adhere to the traditional division of labor.

Cuna men hunt and fish, while the women care for the home and children. Women typically do not leave the settlement, but the men will often leave for years and go to college.

In the Guaymí tribe, women have a subservient role to men and often have to share their husband with other women.

The Chocó tribe, however, elevates the women to a more equal status in society. The women work in the fields and have property rights. While the Chocó society is patrilineal, meaning that children inherit from their father rather than their mother, the men respect the women and include them in making important decisions.

Despite progress in gender roles, many Panamanian women feel that because of traditional roles for men and women in society they have a difficult time earning respect in the workplace and balancing a family and a career.

These two teachers, similar to many of the women in Panama today, are learning to handle their changing gender roles.

LIFE IN THE DARIÉN GAP

Several Indian tribes live in the Darién region amid the dense foliage and wild animals of the Panamanian jungle. Settlements exist along the twisting rivers and mountains of this region. The Darién region is also home to the Chocó Indians and some of the smaller tribes. The Cuna Indians also reside in the Darién jungle and maintain what anthropologists call "the last original democracy on earth."

Living in the Darién jungle is neither luxurious nor easy. The residents battle excruciating heat, wild animals, and swarms of large mosquitos. Although the rivers serve as their principal means of transport, navigating through tangled vines and trees is difficult. The residents of the Darién rely upon the plants and animals of the region for food and resources but occasionally venture out of the region to acquire modern goods. They build their homes from trees, sticks, grass, and leaves.

The Indians are friendly to the occasional visitor, but visitors will not convince them to adopt modern ways. Skilled artisans who make beautiful baskets, carvings, and necklaces, the Chocós will sell their items to visitors but prefer to exchange them for a pair of blue jeans, sneakers, flashlights, or nylon windbreakers.

PANAMANIAN CHILDREN

Children are an integral part of Panamanian society and Panamanian parents hope for and love their children.

Despite the emerging trend for women to work, most children spend most of their early years with their mothers. In the rural areas, children often live with their parents until they marry; and often they continue to live with one spouse's parents after marriage. In the cities children either remain with their parents until marriage or live on their own in apartments.

Children are also very important to the native tribes. Cuna Indian couples have many children, and the mother is the nurturer. Male children do not wear clothes until they are between 5 and 7 years old. Female children, however, begin wearing the native dresses with molas when they are born. When an infant girl is one month old the Cunas pierce her nose and insert a coconut-soaked thread. After a few days her mother puts a nose ring through the hole, and the child continues to wear larger rings as she grows up.

Panamanian children, especially in the rural areas, grow up near their relatives and learn early in life the importance of the family.

EDUCATION

Panamanian law requires that children between the ages of 7 and 15 attend primary school. Panama's quality of education has increased dramatically during the past century. In 1923 over 70% of Panamanians were illiterate; today only 12% cannot read.

Education is important to Panamanians. Parents encourage their children to pursue a university education because it enables them to enter the professional job market.

After completing primary school, students may attend one of two types of free secondary schools: the academic-oriented program or the vocational school. Half of Panamanian young adults attend secondary school; almost 75% of them select the academic program, which involves two three-year cycles. During the first cycle, the students take classes in Spanish, religion, art, music, and social studies. The other cycle consists of either more rigorous studies in arts and sciences if the student plans to go on to a university, or a three-year course that completes the student's schooling. Vocational secondary programs teach students technical skills such as agricultural and industrial trades.

Panama has three institutes of higher education. Approximately 75% of university students attend the state-run University of Panama. To attend a university, a student must complete the upper cycle of secondary school and acquire a *bachillerato* ("bah-chee-yay-RAH-toh"), or diploma. For every three eligible candidates, only one secures a place. The university program lasts six years.

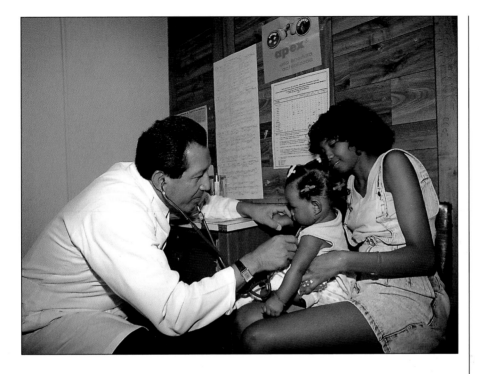

A doctor attends to his young patient at a health center. The physician to patient ratio in Panama is one to 910, which is a drastic improvement over the 2,000 patients per physician ratio in 1960.

HEALTH AND WELFARE

Panamanians enjoy some of the best health care in Latin America. The average life expectancy for males is 71 years and for females 75 years. Panamanians have enjoyed higher health standards over the past few years because the government assumed responsibility for the health care system in the 1970s and gave responsibility for public health to the minister of health in the late 1980s. As a result, rural health care has improved over the past 20 years. A disparity between rural and urban health care continues to exist, however, because advanced medical facilities are concentrated in the cities.

Panama's government spends over $100 million per year on health care, which is 6.6% of total government spending. The Ministry of Health employs medical directors to maintain health care services, health centers, hospitals, and programs at the district and regional levels. The Social Security Institute provides retirement pensions and health care for its members, who include permanent employees who pay taxes to the system.

Under General Torrijos, the Panamanian government drastically improved the public health care system. The government promised "Health for All by the Year 2000" and embarked on a comprehensive program to improve services and sanitation in the rural areas.

61

CITY LIFE

Over the past four decades Panamanians have moved to the cities in droves. Until the 1950s only one-third of Panama's population was urban. Today over 53% of Panama's residents live in the cities. Panama City has a population of over 625,000 people, and Colón has almost 140,000 residents. Three Panamanian cities, David, Santiago, and Penonomé, have between 60,000 and 100,000 residents. Four other cities, Chitré, Chepigana, Las Tablas, and Bocas del Toro, have between 20,000 and 38,000 residents.

The Panama Canal has been one of the factors that encouraged many rural residents to move to the cities: the two largest cities, Panama City and Colón, are located on the canal. These two cities combined have over two-thirds of the urban population.

Panamanian city dwellers live in houses or apartment buildings made of wood or concrete. The wealthier residents live in old colonial houses that have numerous balconies, while the middle class lives in more moderate homes or apartments. The less fortunate residents live in slum communities with thousands of others.

Historically the city dwellers isolated themselves based on wealth, race, and social status. Before the influx of urban migrants over the past few decades, the cities were somewhat segregated. The growth of the cities blurred the distinct lines, and although upper-class sections of the cities still exist, different social classes now live in the same neighborhood.

Life in Panama's cities teems with activity and movement. Most city buildings have corrugated iron or clay tile roofs.

RURAL LIFE

The majority of rural residents are relatively poor; almost 75% of them live below the poverty line. Most of the rural men are herders and farmers, while the women primarily work in their home or as domestic help in another home.

The community spirit is strong in rural society. For instance, rural men often help another family to build a home. Rural families encourage their children to attend school and better themselves.

Although rural life is more primitive than urban life in Panama, the government has instituted health and welfare programs that have benefited the rural communities. These programs have brought more advanced health care and clean water to the villages and towns. The Torrijos government brought other changes to the rural areas when it established collectives and redistributed farmland. Many of the Panamanians who acquired land through this program sold it to wealthy cattle ranchers and migrated to the cities.

A quiet moment in a rural community. Although rural residents are generally poorer, community spirit among them is strong.

A TRIP THROUGH THE PANAMA CANAL

The Panama Canal charges a toll to every ship that passes through it. The average toll for a cruise ship is $30,000. In 1982 the Queen Elizabeth II paid the highest toll ever—$99,065.22. A man named Richard Halliburton paid the lowest toll ever, 36 cents, when he swam across the canal in 1928.

When the United States was building the Panama Canal, the popular slogan was "The Land Divided, A World United." Since the first ship passed through the canal in 1914, the canal has served as a link between the Atlantic and Pacific oceans for ships of all types. Hundreds of cruise ships pass through the canal each year so that tourists may enjoy the magnificent passage through the mountains, lakes, and locks. Ships may pass either way through the canal, which has three sets of parallel locks to handle traffic approaching from either ocean.

A ship that is sailing from the Atlantic to the Pacific Ocean enters the canal through Limón Bay. Before a ship enters the canal, a pilot from the Panama Canal Commission boards the ship to guide it through the canal. The captain navigates the ship into the canal and along a seven-mile passage to the Gatun Locks.

The Gatun Locks are three pairs of concrete chambers, resembling a staircase, that lift the ship to 85 feet (26 meters) above sea level. Each lock chamber is 1,000 feet (305 meters) long and 110 feet (34 meters) wide, which is often about the size of the ship. Six electric locomotives, called mules, run along tracks on both sides of the locks. Attached to the ship, they guide it through the narrow locks. When the ship enters the first lock, canal workers release water from Gatun Lake on the other side of Gatun Locks; this lifts the vessel to the level of the next chamber. This process, which takes about 10 minutes, continues through each of the locks until the ship is at the level of Gatun Lake. Once the ship reaches Gatun Lake, canal workers detach the mules and let the ship enter the lake.

Gatun Lake is a quiet lake with small green islands filled with animals, birds, and flowers. The ship passes through the beautiful Gatun Lake to the Gaillard Cut.

The Gaillard Cut is an eight-mile (12.9-kilometer), man-made channel. Green mountains, which are dotted with wild orchids at certain times of the year, border the channel. At the end of the Gaillard Cut are the Pedro Miguel Locks, which in one step lower the ship 31 feet (10 meters) into Miraflores Lake. After crossing the 1.5-mile (2.5-kilometer) lake, the ship enters the Miraflores Locks.

The Miraflores Locks are two chambers that lower the ship to the level of the Pacific Ocean. The engineers designed two locks at the Pacific end of the canal because they believed that the underlying soil would not support one large lock. When the ship enters the first lock, canal workers release water to the level of the second lock. The second chamber lowers the ship to sea level—which changes twice a day by about 12.5 feet (3.8 meters).

After passing through the Miraflores Locks, the ship travels along another eight-mile (12.9-kilometer) channel toward the end of the canal. Along this channel are the towns of Balboa, Balboa Heights, and La Boca. Hundreds of pleasure boats line this passageway as well. The ship passes under the Bridge of the Americas, and the canal pilot returns the wheel to the captain of the ship. After the ship passes through the Panama Canal it enters the Pacific Ocean.

The Miraflores Locks are probably the most photographed spot in Panama. Because of the varying tides of the Pacific Ocean, the Miraflores Locks have the highest lock gates in the canal.

A typical journey through the 50-mile-long (80.5-kilometer) canal lasts eight hours, but can take as long as 15 hours if the ship has to wait for other ships to pass through the canal.

RELIGION

THE PANAMANIAN Constitution allows citizens to choose their own religion, yet between 85 and 90% of the population is Roman Catholic. The remaining citizens are Protestants, Jews, Muslims, Baha'is, or Hindus. Protestantism is growing and now accounts for approximately 10% of the population. The Indians of Panama have their own religions that are specific to their tribe.

The Spaniards established the Catholic faith as Panama's religion in the 16th century. Since that time Panamanians have continued to follow the religious tenets of the Catholic faith. Because the large majority of the population is Catholic, the canons of this faith permeate both the religious and cultural environment. Devout Catholics visit the church and observe religious duties daily, and the less devout, or liberal, Catholics adhere to the religious calendar.

The Baha'i faith is one of the minority religions of Panama. Despite the small number of Panamanians, one of the religion's seven houses of worship worldwide is located in Panama. The Baha'is believe that all major religions have divine origins, and they accept many of the teachings of Christianity, Islam, Buddhism, Hinduism, and Judaism. The Baha'is are devout and visit their house of worship often. Preachers do not lead their religious worships because they believe that humans cannot know God.

Opposite: **The Black Christ in Portobelo is believed to have saved the town from a cholera epidemic.**

Below: **This Catholic woman holds a candle as an offering to the Virgin Mary.**

The golden altar at the Church of San José in Panama City. A resourceful monk thwarted an attempt by Henry Morgan to steal it by painting the altar black.

Almost all Panamanian heads of government have been Roman Catholics.

THE CONSTITUTION AND RELIGION

Panama's Constitution provides for freedom of religion, meaning that the citizens may follow any faith, or no faith, and the government will not interfere. A citizen may not be punished for professing an unusual religion or forming a new religion. The constitution also prohibits the government from discriminating against religious groups. Each religion is entitled to the same protection under the law.

Panama does not have a state religion, but Roman Catholicism is the predominant faith. The constitution provides that schools may, but do not have to, instruct students on Roman Catholicism. Panama's Constitution, unlike the U.S. Constitution, does not require separation of church and state.

The constitution prohibits members of the clergy from holding public office in the country, unless the office relates to social assistance, education, or scientific research. It requires senior officials of the church hierarchy to be native-born Panamanians. The constitution allows foreign clergy who enter Panama to enjoy the same religious freedoms as Panamanian citizens. This means that, unlike other members of the clergy who are Panamanian citizens, foreign clergy may hold public office but cannot be senior members of the church.

RELIGIOUS HOLIDAYS

Many of Panama's national holidays are religious. Easter and Christmas are the most important ones, but the other ones also have religious significance to the people. The other religious holidays are: Shrove Tuesday, which is the Tuesday before Ash Wednesday; Maundy Thursday; Good Friday; All Souls' Day; and Immaculate Conception Day.

CATHEDRALS

Panama is the home of many beautiful places of worship, and many of the churches were built during Spanish colonial days. In addition to Catholic churches, Panama has places of worship for Protestants, Muslims, Hindus, and Baha'is. Panama's oldest church is located in Nata, a town along the Gulf of Panama. The Spaniards built this church in 1520, and Catholics still worship at this beautiful, old church.

When the buccaneer Henry Morgan attacked the old Panama City, he destroyed many beautiful churches as well as most of the city. He burned the cathedral, but an imposing belfry tower still remains, as do some of the walls. On his rampage through Panama, Morgan demolished many buildings and stole gold and priceless items.

Panama City's largest cathedral is the Metropolitan Cathedral. Many interesting events have occurred at this cathedral. When Omar Torrijos died, the viewing of his body and his

The Plaza Cathedral in Panama City, one of the many churches that are found in Panama.

funeral were held here. In 1990 President Endara fasted at the church for almost two weeks to protest the lack of financial aid from the United States following the 1989 invasion to overthrow Noriega. The president wanted to show the poor people of Panama that he understood their plight, and he wanted to spur the United States to action.

69

RELIGIOUS BELIEFS OF THE INDIANS

RELIGIOUS BELIEFS OF THE CUNA INDIANS Although some Cunas practice the Catholic faith, the majority retain ancestral tribal beliefs. Ritual

A Cuna child wearing a monkey teeth necklace.

plays an important role in the Cuna faith, and members of the tribe gain prestige through their knowledge of ritual. The Cuna believe that all living things have a spirit that should be respected and protected.

An important Cuna ritual is the *inna-nega* ("een-NAH nay-GAH"), or "coming-out" party, for young women. When a girl reaches puberty, the tribe celebrates the event with a three-day celebration. Before the ritual, the young woman's female relatives decide on a special mola that they will all wear. These women secretly make the molas, which may become popular throughout the Cuna region that year. On the first two days of the celebration, the women serve food and drink. The *kantules* ("kahn-TOO-lay"), or priests, sit in a ceremonial house, and the tribe chants stories about the history of the Cunas. On the third day of the festivities, the women join in and the tribe bestows a permanent name upon the young woman and cuts her hair.

The Cunas believe that they enter another life after death. To achieve honor in the next life, they strive to reach a high level in their current life. One way to achieve a high status is to collect the teeth of the white-faced monkey, a fierce animal. The Cunas kill the monkey and put its teeth on a necklace. The more monkeys a Cuna kills, the longer the necklace. The Cunas believe that they will be rewarded in their next life if they had a long necklace of monkey teeth during their life on earth.

RELIGIOUS BELIEFS OF THE CHOCÓ INDIANS The Chocó Indians, despite visits from religious missionaries, continue to worship their own gods. The men carve ritual sculptures and altars to their gods. When Chocós are sick, they first try to cure themselves with medicinal plants. If this treatment is unsuccessful, they seek the help of one of the tribe's *jabaina* ("ha-bah-EE-nah"), or medicine men, who calls upon the gods for assistance.

The Chocó Indians have remained steadfast to their own faith despite attempts to convert them to Christianity.

Chocó men usually wear only a loin cloth held up by a string tied around their waists. For religious ceremonies and other festivities, the men wear multicolored woven pants, a beaded chestplate, hammered silver crowns, earrings, and bracelets. From their ankles to their lower lips, Chocós paint themselves with a black pigment extracted from the seeds of a local fruit. They apply the pigment in elaborate patterns; it lasts for about 10 days.

The Chocó women, who usually wear dresses or other suitable clothes for the warm weather, also have a special costume for religious events. They roll a brilliantly-colored cloth around their hips; it goes to their knees, like a skirt. They usually do not wear a shirt or blouse for these events and are bare-breasted except for beaded necklaces. The women also decorate their skin with black pigment.

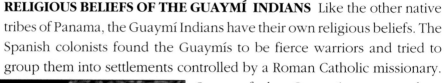

In the 20th century, Protestant missionaries have
been successful in con-
verting some of the
Guaymí Indians to their
faith.

RELIGIOUS BELIEFS OF THE GUAYMÍ INDIANS Like the other native tribes of Panama, the Guaymí Indians have their own religious beliefs. The Spanish colonists found the Guaymís to be fierce warriors and tried to group them into settlements controlled by a Roman Catholic missionary.

Some of the Guaymís converted to Christianity, but most of them rebelled against the Spanish control and moved to remote areas of the country.

The Guaymí religion is ritualistic, and music and celebrations are an important part of their religion. The Guaymís make their own instruments out of animal bones, large sea shells, turtle shells, wood, and animal skins. During religious events and other festivities, men and women paint different designs on their faces and file their incisor teeth into sharp points that resemble fangs.

One of the most important rituals in the Guaymí culture is the *guro* ("GOO-roh"), which occurs when a boy reaches puberty. Unlike the Cuna inna-nega, the guro is a mysterious ritual to which only the men are privy. The elders of the tribe take the young man into the jungle and make him complete difficult physical tests to prove his endurance. The elders chant as the young man undergoes the tests.

PANAMANIAN MYTHS

Panamanians have many myths and legends that they tell to their children. One famous myth is called "La Luz del Llano," meaning "the light of the field." According to this myth, people who lived in the Panamanian town of Santiago de Veraguas would see a light shining over one of the fields. However, when the residents walked into the field, the light disappeared. They interpreted the light to mean that they should build a college to train schoolteachers. Thus, the light symbolized enlightening education.

Panamanians and tourists also are familiar with the famous myth of the haunted house by the Bridge of the Americas, which crosses the Panama Canal. According to the myth, a man killed a female visitor to his house by chopping off her head. The man then buried the woman under the floor of his house. Believers claim that a headless woman now haunts this small house on the Panamanian side of the Bridge of the Americas.

Another famous myth among Panamanians is the legend of Belisario Porras. Mr. Porras, a famous Panamanian political leader, fled from his enemies during a war. With his enemies in close pursuit, Mr. Porras arrived at "la luz del llano" in a field near Santiago de Veraguas. When he reached the field, however, the light did not disappear. Rather, a tall woman wearing a full peasant skirt appeared in the light. Mr. Porras asked if he could hide from his enemies under her skirt, and she agreed. When his enemies arrived at the field, they did not see him. Thus he survived the wrath of his enemies, thanks to this generous woman in the lighted field.

The Guaymí religion does not forbid polygamy, and some of the men have several wives. The Guaymí who have converted to Christianity, however, are monogamous.

FOLK AND OTHER RELIGIOUS BELIEFS

Rural Panamanians have unique folk beliefs that they share with some urban Panamanians, primarily those who have migrated to the cities. Although the rural Panamanians are Roman Catholic, their folk beliefs integrate with their religious ones to deviate from the basic tenets of Catholicism. The folklore places God, the Devil, the Virgin Mary, and saints at the center of the belief system. The believers view Jesus Christ as the chief saint, but do not centralize him as the Catholic faith does. Women admire the Virgin Mary and try to emulate her actions and beliefs.

Even if a person has not been a devout Catholic, a priest often will administer last rites anyway. This tradition is important to those who believe that they will appear before the Devil and God on All Souls' Day, because their last contact on earth was with a religious figure.

TEACHING RELIGION TO BOYS AND GIRLS

Parents teach religious beliefs to their children at an early age, and mothers frequently take their children to daily mass. Most Panamanian children celebrate their first communion by the age of 10. Interestingly, most young men distance themselves from the church as they grow older. Throughout their lives, many men do not attend church on a regular basis, but they continue to consider themselves Roman Catholics. Because all of the Catholic clergy are men, some male Panamanians obviously remain involved with the Church.

Parents and the Catholic Church encourage young women to remain involved in the church and devoted to the religion after they take their first communion. Women of both rural and urban areas usually become involved in church social events.

ALL SOULS' DAY

To rural Panamanians, the Devil represents the evil that can alter their destiny, which is set by God. According to folklore, the Devil constantly entices humans to live with him in the afterlife by offering them almost irresistible things on earth. When a person dies, Saint Peter will use a Roman balance scale to weigh the person's good and bad deeds. If the good deeds outweigh the bad, the person will spend the afterlife in Heaven. If not, then the person will go to Hell. The weighing process occurs annually on All Souls' Day. On this day, God and the Devil summon before them everyone who died in the previous year. People who have not yet died spend All Souls' Day reviewing their own lives. Even urban Panamanians, who do not necessarily believe all of the folk tales, consider All Souls' Day to be an important day of reverence and reflection.

At a funeral in Veraguas
Province, mourners gath-
er round to view the body.

BIRTH AND DEATH

Folk believers place great importance on birth and death, and they
commemorate these events with religious liturgies. Baptism is the most
significant religious ceremony as it symbolizes the infant's entry into
society and the church. Rural Panamanians believe so strongly in the
importance of baptism that entire families often travel for miles to a parish
center. A child's first communion also is an important event. Children
attend classes to prepare them for their first communion and subsequent
involvement in the church.

Death also is an important event that Panamanians mark with a
religious ceremony. The family of the deceased has the body embalmed
and then places it on display for mourners to view. After a few days of
visits, the family holds services in the church or place of worship. The
mourners then form a procession and follow those carrying the casket to
the grave site.

The Virgin Mary is an important figure in the Roman Catholic faith.

HISTORY OF ROMAN CATHOLICISM IN PANAMA

The first European settlers in Panama, the Spanish, were Roman Catholics, and they brought their religion to Panama. Pedrarias the Cruel organized the Catholic religion in Panama according to the laws of the church. He thwarted the native tribes' rebellions and tried to convert the tribes to Christianity.

At the end of the 18th century, the Roman Catholic church established the first bishopric, or office of bishop, on the American continent in Panama City. Unfortunately, Henry Morgan destroyed the cathedral that housed the first American diocese on his rampage in 1671. For almost 400 years Panama followed the Roman Catholic faith of Spain. By the time Panama declared its independence from Spain, Roman Catholicism was ingrained in the people, and it remains the most popular religion in the country today.

RITUALS AND BELIEFS OF THE ROMAN CATHOLIC FAITH

According to Christians, Jesus Christ established a church that was to encompass all races, cultures, and nations. He called this church "catholic." The Catholic Church, as it is known today, retained the "catholic" title because it was the only all-encompassing and universal church in the early centuries of Christianity. Catholics believe that popes, bishops, and priests are the successors of Jesus' apostles and are placed on earth to spread the word of God.

The Bible represents God's word to Christians. The Old Testament of the Bible tells the story of God forming the Old Covenant with the Hebrew people. The New Testament tells the story of God's work through Jesus Christ. In the 1500s, the Catholic faith was floundering as the Protestant Reformation drew many believers away from the Catholic church. Since Spain remained a Catholic nation, however, Panama, as its colony, became Catholic as well.

Panamanian Catholics have many religious beliefs that are exclusive to their country. For instance, Catholics from all over the country worship the Black Christ. An 18th century church in Portobelo contains a life-size wooden sculpture called the Black Christ. Every October 21, hundreds of worshippers visit the statue. Most of the worshippers wear purple garments like the ones that adorn the statue. The most devout worshippers attach gold charms to their garments as symbols of their faith.

In addition to religious festivals, Christmas and Easter are the two most important religious holidays for Panamanian Catholics. Another important day is the Day of the Immaculate Conception. On this day, Panamanians honor the Virgin Mary. At the same time, they also honor their own mothers.

An important ritual for Panamanian Catholics is the Holy Week Processional. This parade occurs during the week before Easter and recalls Jesus Christ's last days on earth, his death, and his resurrection.

LANGUAGE

THE OFFICIAL LANGUAGE of Panama is Spanish, but so many Panamanians speak English that the country may be considered bilingual. Panamanians are fluent in English as well as Spanish because of the U.S. presence in the Canal Zone. The Afro-Caribbeans, who originally came to Panama from the West Indies, have retained their English tongue as well. Over 80% of the population speak Spanish as the native language, and a large majority of this group speak English as well. Fourteen percent of the population speak English as their native tongue.

The native tribes have their own dialects. The Cuna Indians speak both Spanish and their native tongue, Cuna. The Cuna Indians speak quickly and accent the last syllable of a word. While speaking, they often stop to give the listener a chance to agree or disagree with what they are saying. The Guaymí Indians speak a language called Morere, or "language of the plains." Over 50% of the Guaymís speak Morere and Spanish, while the remaining speak only Spanish. Embera is the native tongue of the Chocó Indians. When Rubén Blades ran for president in the 1994 elections, he formed a political party called Papa Egoro. This phrase comes from the Embera language and means "Mother Earth."

Other Panamanians, such as the East Indians and Chinese, who do not speak Spanish, English, or an indigenous language, speak the native tongues of the countries from which they came. For the most part, however, Panamanians speak Spanish or Spanish and English.

Opposite: **With literacy in Panama at a high of 88%, reading is a popular pastime.**

Below: **Billboards are a common medium of political propaganda. During his rule, Omar Torrijos used billboards to communicate his concern for his country and people.**

Lo que yo quiero para Mis Hijos, Lo quiero para Mi Pueblo.

TORRIJOS

Approximately 500,000 Panamanian homes and businesses own a television, and over 255,000 residents purchase one of the five major daily newspapers per day.

THE SPANISH LANGUAGE

The Spanish alphabet has 28 letters: *a, b, c, ch, d, e, f, g, h i, j, l, ll, m, n, ñ, o, p, q, r, rr, s, t, u, v, x, y,* and *z*. The Spanish alphabet does not contain the English letters *k* or *w*. Some words of foreign origin, such as *kilo* and *kilómetro*, use the letter *k*. Otherwise, the Spanish letter *c* sounds like the English *k* unless *e* or *i* follows it (then it sounds like the English *s*).

Like the English alphabet, the Spanish one has five vowels that the letters *a, e, i, o,* and *u* represent. Each vowel has one basic sound:

a	is pronounced like the *a* in *father*
e	is pronounced like the *ai* in *train*
i	is pronounced like the *ee* in *teeth*
o	is pronounced like the *o* in *slow*
u	is pronounced like the *u* in *dude*

Spanish words can be stressed on the last, second to last, or third to last syllable. If the stress is on the last syllable, it only carries a written accent if it ends in a vowel, *s*, or *n*. If the stress is on the second to last syllable, it only carries a written accent if the word does *not* end in a vowel, *s*, or, *n*. If the stress is on the third to last syllable it carries a written accent in all cases.

Many of the consonants of the Spanish language are similar to their English counterparts. Some of the notable differences are:

1. *b* and *v* are interchangeable. If a word begins with either a *b* or a *v*, it sounds like the *b* in *boy*. If either letter falls in the middle or the end of a sentence, it is pronounced like the *v* in *devil*.
2. *d* sounds like its English counterpart unless it is between two vowels. Then, it sounds like the *th* in *thank*.
3. *g* sounds like the *g* in *girl*. If an *e* or *i* follows a *g*, however, then it sounds like *h* in *hello*.
4. *h* is silent in Spanish.
5. *j* sounds like the English *h* as in *house*.
6. *ll*, which is a single letter in the Spanish language, is pronounced as an English *y*, as in *yellow*.
7. *ñ* sounds like the *ny* in *canyon*.
8. *r*, in Spanish, is a slightly rolled, but very quickly spoken letter.
9. *rr* is the *r* sound strongly trilled.
10. *z* resembles the English *s* in *song*.

THE PRESS

Panama has five major daily newspapers, four commercial television stations, one educational television station run by the University of Panama, one educational television station associated with the Catholic Church, and over 100 radio stations.

The leading newspaper in Panama is called *La Prensa*, meaning The Press. It has a circulation of 50,000. The other major daily papers are *Crítica Libre*, with a circulation of 30,000; *El Siglo*, *La Estrella de Panama*, and *El Panama America*, each with 25,000 daily readers. In 1990, a right-wing political group began a daily newspaper called the *Primera Plana*.

Street vendors selling *La Prensa*, the leading local newspaper. The major newspapers in Panama are in Spanish. The English-language daily papers are *The Star* and *The Herald*.

The Panamanian press provides a wide array of information to the citizens, including international and domestic news, political commentaries, editorials, and special features. Although the law allows some freedom of the press, it does provide that journalists may be immediately disciplined for showing disrespect to certain government officials.

The media and the government historically have been at odds in Panama. A journalist and government opponent, Roberto Eisenmann, lived in exile in the United States during the Noriega era because he feared that the government was conspiring to kill him. President Endara reinstated freedom of the press after the Noriega regime forced many domestic and foreign media personnel to leave the country.

Panamanians consider it rude if people do not engage in small talk, use obliging words, and properly address and leave a group of people.

GREETINGS

Panamanians are polite people with considerate greetings and formalities in their everyday life. For instance, a business person always makes small talk with a colleague or client before discussing business. Panamanians are

offended if anyone initiates a business conversation before spending time to learn about the other party on a personal level. Panamanians of either sex may greet each other by shaking hands. Women friends typically kiss each other on one cheek when greeting and departing. Men and women sometimes kiss each other on the cheek, but two men always shake hands. The tradition of kissing on one cheek differs from the South American tradition of kissing another person on both cheeks. Usually the kiss is an "air-kiss," and the people do not actually place their lips on the other's cheek.

Panamanians are very gracious and polite. They frequently say "please" (*por favor*), "thank you" (*gracias*), and "you're welcome" (*de nada*). Before joining a group of people who are eating or conversing, a newcomer will ask permission to join the group by saying *con permiso* ("kohn pair-MEE-soh"). The group responds by saying *andele* ("AHN-day-lay"), which means "go ahead."

CONVERSATION

One of the major taboos in Panamanian conversation, which differs from the United States, is a discussion of personal possessions. Unlike persons of other nations, Panamanians are not interested in discussing status and money with each other. Another topic that Panamanians do not like to discuss, especially with U.S. citizens, is the building of the canal and the U.S. intervention. Panamanians generally do not like to discuss local politics and race in social settings. The favorite topics of conversation among Panamanians are family, common friends, hobbies, interests, and sports such as basketball and baseball.

In social interaction, Panamanians are careful not to discuss personal topics such as money or material possessions.

NONVERBAL COMMUNICATION

An important part of Panamanian communication is nonverbal behavior and gestures. While many of the gestures are similar to those in the United States, some are worthy of mention.

Shaking hands when meeting someone shows good manners and can be done in two ways: either the standard American handshake, or palm to palm with the thumb facing toward the person (like an arm wrestling position). When Panamanians want another person to approach them, they will raise one of their hands with their palm facing the other person. This gesture resembles the North American wave.

A recent census showed that some Panamanians name their children after dictators or commercial products.

Panamanians call both their country and their capital city Panamá. *This common reference often is confusing to foreigners.*

PANAMANIAN NAMES

Panamanians have two surnames after their first name. The first is the father's name, and the second the mother's. Thus, if a child is named Ana María and her mother's name is Chavez and her father's name is Gonzalez, her name will be Ana María Gonzalez Chavez. In formal situations, Panamanians will use the second surname. Thus, Ana María would go by Ana María Chavez on formal occasions.

When a couple marries, the woman adds her husband's first surname, that of his father, to her own first surname. A woman keeps her own first surname to honor her family and pass the name along to her children. The word *de*, meaning "of," precedes her husband's surname. If Ana María marries a man named Juan Federico Nuñez Alvarez, her new name will be either Ana María de Nuñez or Ana María Gonzalez de Nuñez. Her husband, Juan, will retain his name, and their children will use Nuñez as the first surname and Gonzalez as the second surname.

THE ORAL TRADITION OF STORYTELLING

Panamanian children look forward to the Feast of All Souls' Day, which is the equivalent of the U.S. Halloween. Traditionally on All Souls' Day, a group of children gather around an adult who tells superstitious tales and frightening stories. Usually the adult will claim to have witnessed whatever event occurs in the story.

The storyteller usually begins the story by asking the children if they have taken care of their familiars, which are invisible beings that surround people. If the children take care of their familiars by paying them attention, the familiars will remain good. However, if the children neglect their familiars, the invisible beings may become evil.

After the first question, the storyteller draws the children in by altering her tone of voice, pausing at important moments, and using hand gestures. The children often become so enthralled by the story that they huddle around the storyteller and hang on her every word. Usually, their eyes are transfixed on the storyteller, not only because they are intrigued by the story but also because they fear that evil spirits might be lurking behind their backs.

The stories are suspenseful, frightening, and often so gruesome that the youngest listeners cover their ears. The storytelling represents an important oral tradition to Panamanians, and children will retell the stories that they heard to their own children. Storytelling is a bonding experience for Panamanian adults and children because they spend time together without modern distractions such as television or radio.

Panama is a Latin American country, and Panamanians refer to their region as Latinoamérica. *They call all of the Spanish-speaking countries of the Americas* Hispanoamérica *and the people* hispanoamericanos.

FORMS OF ADDRESS

Panamanians address others based on the person's social status and familiarity. While the English language has one word for the second person ("you"), Spanish has two words: the familiar *tu* or the formal *usted*. When Panamanians meet a person who is the same age or older, they refer to the person as *usted*. As they become friends, they call each other *tu*. When meeting a younger person for the first time, a Panamanian usually uses *tu* unless the younger person is prestigious. Persons of lower class almost always will call a person of higher status *usted*.

ARTS

PANAMA HAS AN extensive folk culture that reflects Spanish, African, North American, and West Indian influences. Panama has wonderful galleries and museums that display some of this folk culture and art.

Not only do museums house the arts, but city buses do as well. The Panamanians purchase yellow school buses from the United States and turn them into wonderfully decorated modes of transportation called *chivas* ("CHEE-vahs"). The art of painting buses began after World War II, and the buses have become the center of much literature in Panama. The artists decorate the buses by first hiding the yellow color under layers of paint. They paint long images, such as a mermaid, a panoramic scene, or a dragon on the side of the bus. The rear emergency door of the bus is the crux of the art, and the artist devotes most of the time to this area. The subject of the door is rarely political, but is often religious.

Some of Panama's oldest and richest art might be buried under the sea. During the 17th century, several ships carrying enormous amounts of treasure such as gold, silver, pearls, and emeralds looted from the early Indian civilizations disappeared into the sea. Christopher Columbus lost four ships in the area of Panama that not only carried treasure, but also, if found and salvaged, would provide examples of ship technology of that period. Although these treasures technically belong to Spain, maritime archaeologists believe that they are located in the sea near Panama. These treasures, if found, would help historians and archaeologists understand the origins of Panamanian art.

Opposite: **The intricately embroidered molas are a major source of income for the Cuna Indians.**

Above: **The buses, or** *chivas,* **in Panama's city streets have brightly painted panels, and no two are alike. Here a bus carries an anti-drug message.**

HISTORICAL BACKGROUND

Panamanian art and literature reflect the state of the country, both politically and culturally. Because Spain and then Colombia controlled Panama before its independence in the early 20th century, the art from these times exhibits the influences of these two countries. When the colonists arrived in Panama, they not only killed thousands of native Indians, but they also destroyed the indigenous art. In building the cities, the colonists refrained from using any Indian-influenced styles. The art from the colonial period mimics the Spanish style and is religious in nature.

Around the 17th century, Panamanians began to reject the Spanish influence and develop a culture of their own. During this time, many great artists, authors, and poets emerged. These artists imitated contemporary art from European countries other than Spain. African art influenced Panamanian art during this period because of the number of African slaves in the country.

When Panama finally became independent in the early 20th century, the artists and authors incorporated indigenous art into their works. The molas of the Cunas became world renowned, and the country no longer squelched primitive artistic expressions of art. Rather, Panamanians were proud of their indigenous art, as well as their success in literature, ballet, and sculpture.

Art finds expression on the walls of a house in Colón.

LITERATURE

The Spanish colonists were the first people to write about Panama. Basilio de Oviedo, Antonio de Herrara, and Pedro de Anglería were three of the best known writers of the early colonial period.

Victor de la Guardia wrote the first Panamanian play at the beginning of the 18th century. After Panama's independence from Spain in the 19th century, many great authors and poets wrote about this important political era, among them Ramón Valdes and Ricardo Miró. Ramón Valdes published *Independence of the Isthmus of Panama*, which discussed Panama separating from Colombia and became the foundation of many subsequent historical treatises. Ricardo Miró was Panama's greatest poet, and one of his poems, "Patria," aroused a feeling of national unity in Panamanians of all ages.

Many of Panama's great literary figures have been political figures as well. Former President Ricardo Alfaro was a Panamanian author, as was General Torrijos's closest aid, José de Jesús Martinez. Martinez, whom the English author Graham Greene portrayed as "Sergeant Chuchu" in *Getting to Know the General*, has won many literary awards.

A Cuna Indian drama group reenacting the death of the Spanish conquerors.

In honor of Ricardo Miró's contribution to Panama's literature, Panama City named a school after him, and a prestigious award, the Premio Ricardo Miró, is given every year to outstanding authors.

89

A folk dance performed to rhythmic music shows a Spanish influence.

SONG AND DANCE

Song and dance are a significant part of Panama's culture. Panamanians enjoy rock music from the United States and England, salsa music, and traditional folk music. The *mejorana* ("may-hoh-RAH-na") is an example of a traditional Panamanian folk song and is either vocal or instrumental. Common instruments that accompany the mejorana are five-stringed guitars called the *bocana* ("boh-KAHN-ah") and the *mejoranera* ("may-hor-ah-NAY-rah"). The mejorana originated in Spain in the 18th century.

The national dance of Panama is the *tamborito* ("tam-boh-REE-toh"), but this dance differs from region to region. The tamborito originated in Spain in the 17th century, but the Panamanian version integrates African rhythms. The dancers perform the tamborito to clapping hands and pounding drums.

Another popular folk dance of Panama is the *cumbia* ("KOOM-byah"), which came to Panama around the time of the African slave trade. Couples who perform this dance form a circle with the other dancers and rotate to the sound of drums and *maracas* ("mah-RAH-kas"), pebble-filled gourds. The dance imitates the Spanish colonists' behavior during the slave trade era.

When performing folk dances, the dancers usually wear elaborate costumes. Because of the strong African influence on the dances themselves, the dancers often wear traditional African apparel. The dancers also wear a lot of gold and pearl jewelry, borrowing some of the designs from the native tribes. If the dancers choose not to wear African costumes, they will wear the traditional Panamanian costumes for men and women.

SALSA AND RUBÉN BLADES

The world is familiar with Panama's salsa music. Salsa music, which originated in Latin America and has spread throughout the world, is an upbeat music that blends rock, jazz, and rhythm and blues with Cuban rhythms.

Rubén Blades, the renowned "King of Salsa," grew up in a poor neighborhood of Panama City. He began his singing career as a neighborhood band leader and by singing jingles for Panamanian beer commercials. When Manuel Noriega accused Blades' father of being a CIA agent, the family left for exile in Miami, Florida.

Blades joined his family in Florida after completing his law degree in Panama. He then moved to New York City to become a professional musician and eventually earned international fame as a salsa singer. After achieving success in the music world, he earned a master's degree at Harvard University and then went to Hollywood to make movies.

Throughout his many careers, Rubén Blades has remained true to his homeland and often writes songs about the common people struggling with poverty. Many Panamanians compare Blades to Bruce Springstein because of his contribution to music and his choice of materials for his music.

In 1994, Rubén Blades returned to Panama to form a new political party and run for president. He was unsuccessful in his bid for the presidency. His next move is unknown, but his fans hope he will continue to make wonderful music in honor of his country and to the delight of salsa lovers all over the world.

Rubén Blades has acted in movies such as "The Super" and "The Milagro Beanfield War."

Restoration work on a colonial building in Panama City.

ARCHITECTURE

Panama has a variety of architecture ranging from Spanish colonial to modern skyscrapers of glass. Rural houses and buildings are built to minimize the effect of the hot tropical sun and maximize the breezes to avoid stagnant, moist air. Panama City has the widest assortment of architectural styles, which give the city a unique, eclectic look.

The current Panama City is actually the second Panama City; Henry Morgan burned the first one to the ground. Panamanians rebuilt the city in a more secure area a few miles away. Today, buildings that are over 300 years old stand in the old Panama City. The older portions of the city resemble Spanish colonial towns, featuring stucco, wrought-iron work, abundant balconies, and cobblestone streets. The newer portions of Panama are filled with sleek boulevards, magnificent glass and concrete highrises, and large tenement housing facilities.

One of the most striking buildings in Panama City is the Presidential Palace with its Moorish balconies decorated with mother-of-pearl. Surrounding the palace are beautiful gardens, and the highlight is the internal courtyard's gardens and fountains.

The Spanish influence can be seen in the buildings in the colonial section of Panama City.

PANAMA CITY'S MUSEUMS

Panama City's culture is as varied as its architecture. In addition to gambling casinos and racetracks, Panama City is home to several wonderful museums. The Queen Torres of Arauz Anthropological Museum displays relics of the Spanish occupation, vestiges of cultures that predate Columbus's arrival, and archaeological artifacts from the hundreds of Indian tribes that inhabited the region.

Another impressive museum is the Museum of the Panamanian Man. This museum provides a history of the country from precolonial times to the building of the Panama Canal and beyond. It has impressive history, archaeology, and anthropology collections.

THE VISUAL ARTS

The Spanish influenced Panamanian sculpture and painting for many centuries. Until the 19th century artists used a baroque style to paint mostly Christian scenes. Today, artists usually depict the sea, landscapes, or the pollera in their paintings. Juan M. Cedeño is the best known Panamanian artist, and other famous painters include Roberto Lewis, Rogelio Sinan, and José G. Mora.

A contemporary Panamanian artist who has been very successful is Sheila Lichacz. She is famous for paintings of tropical fruits, sea shells, and *tinajas* ("teen-AH-has"), which are large earthen jars. Her work honors ancient cultures of Panama, nature, and religious traditions. Her paintings have, in the last decade, earned her status as a great Latin American artist, and museums around the world display her art. One of her most famous series of paintings, called *Infinity*, depicts the relationship of nature and culture, and God and the artist.

The native tribes contribute to Panama's visual arts as well. Their ancestors produced the sculptures of the pre-Colombian period; today, the tribes continue to produce beautiful artifacts and paintings. In addition to making molas, the Cuna Indians create sculpture, clay pottery, and baskets. The Guaymí Indians make for sale exquisite jewelry crafted from bones, shells, or glass. The specialty of the Guaymís is the *chaquira* ("chah-KEE-rah"), which is a multicolored beaded necklace.

A three-legged pre-Colombian pot from Chiriquí Province. Each of its hollow legs has a ball that rolls up and down and a lizard figure on top.

MOLAS

Mola literally means "cloth," but to the Cuna Indians, the mola is the beautiful and intricately appliquéd panel of a blouse. Cuna women have been making molas for hundreds of years, and in the past century mola production has become a major industry and source of income for the tribe. Today the molas are used not only for the traditional Cuna costume, but also for blouses, cushions, and wall coverings.

The Cunas believe that all things have a spirit, so the mola maker takes great pride in creating a spirit for her mola. Each mola has an original theme or motif. In creating a mola, the maker relies upon her thoughts, her religion, and her environment to design a pattern. She often integrates many things into her design, such as animals, insects, birds, plants, religious scenes, and legends; or her design might be abstract. Common themes of the mola design are world events, religious scenery, and flora and fauna of the country, including the Canal region. Some Cuna designs are passed down from one generation to the next.

The Cuna tribe expects women to be good mola makers, and the women begin to teach the girls at a young age how to make beautiful molas. In this way the women hand down their intricate sewing skills from one generation to the next. If a girl does not become an adept mola maker, the medicine man will hold a special ceremony in which he burns certain herbs to make her become one. A young Cuna woman usually offers her future husband about 24 molas as her dowry.

The average mola is 16 by 24 inches (41 by 61 centimeters) in size. Despite the relatively small size, most mola makers spend several months securing the layers of the panel with tiny stitches. The process of making a mola is quite elaborate: first the maker stacks and bastes together two to seven layers of colored fabric and draws or visualizes the design on the top piece. Then, she cuts out various designs to reveal the colored layers underneath. Finally, after all of the cutting, she adds final details with embroidery or appliqué. The end result is a beautiful and colorful mola that she may keep for herself or sell for a profit.

LEISURE

THE VARIED TOPOGRAPHY of Panama enables its citizens to enjoy a variety of leisure activities.

THE SPORTING LIFE

The mountains of Panama provide a haven for fitness enthusiasts. Hikers tackle the Volcán Barú, Panama's highest mountain. Many parts of the mountain are too steep for hiking, but some Panamanians go mountain and rock climbing. The Volcán Barú is dormant, so many guides offer exploration treks through the crater. There are several thermal springs and cool lagoons in the mountains. The many rivers and streams supply adventures in white-water rafting and fishing. Hunting and bird-watching in the mountains are popular with some Panamanians.

One of the more interesting water activities in Panama is exploring Gatun Lake. This lake, which was built to accommodate the Panama Canal, is the second largest artificial lake in the world.

Opposite: **Local children enjoying a dip in the sea.**

Left: **Bird-watching is popular with tourists.**

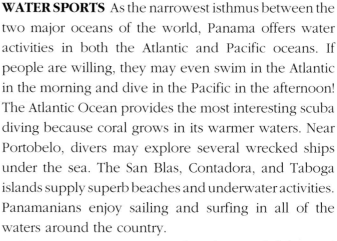

WATER SPORTS As the narrowest isthmus between the two major oceans of the world, Panama offers water activities in both the Atlantic and Pacific oceans. If people are willing, they may even swim in the Atlantic in the morning and dive in the Pacific in the afternoon! The Atlantic Ocean provides the most interesting scuba diving because coral grows in its warmer waters. Near Portobelo, divers may explore several wrecked ships under the sea. The San Blas, Contadora, and Taboga islands supply superb beaches and underwater activities. Panamanians enjoy sailing and surfing in all of the waters around the country.

Panama's name means "abundance of fish," and fishing enthusiasts can catch an abundance of fish off Panamanian shores. Panama is known to fish lovers as "the black marlin capital of the world." Other popular fish to catch are striped marlin, dolphin, roosterfish, wahoo, and rainbow runners. Gatun Lake provides excellent freshwater bass fishing.

NATIONAL SPECTATOR SPORTS The most popular spectator sports in Panama are baseball, basketball, soccer, boxing, horse racing, cockfighting, and dog racing. Baseball is the national sport, and Panamanians love both to play and to watch this sport. Like citizens of the United States, Panamanians enjoy watching the World Series. Panamanians also enjoy soccer; but unlike their neighbor, Colombia, they do not consider soccer to be the national sport.

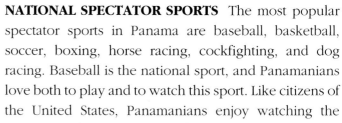

THE BALSERÍA

The Guaymí Indians' most significant festivity is a game called the *balsería* ("bahl-say-REE-ah"). This game originated long before the Spanish colonists arrived in Panama, and many of the Guaymís still play it today. Because the game is extremely violent, the Pananamian government passed a law declaring it illegal for citizens to partake in the balsería. This law, along with the brutal nature of the game, has deterred some groups of Guaymís who have banned it from their culture.

Balsería is a game played between two different Guaymí tribes. The chief of one tribe initiates the play by challenging another tribe to fight. The challenge is formal: the chief sends members of the tribe who carry several knotted strings (the number of knots designates the number of days until balsería). If the tribe accepts the fight, they keep the strings. Then the two tribes meet to fight each other and celebrate. During the fight, the men of the opposing tribes fight each other with tree logs or sticks called *balsos* ("BAHL-sohs").

The tribe that challenged the other tribe hosts the fight. Before the opponent arrives, the host prepares drinks, chooses an open field for the fight, and builds huts for the opponents. The night before the fight, the opponents arrive with painted faces, stuffed game animals tied to their shoulders, and fancy hats. They bring their wives with them and announce their arrival with loud, obnoxious music. Both tribes stay awake all night, and many participants drink an abundance of alcohol.

The following morning the balsería begins. Because the men fight with long sticks and aim to injure each other, many players are killed or seriously injured. Most of the Guaymís are drunk for the balsería, including the women, who often begin to fight with each other. When the balsería finally ends, the women sing a mournful farewell song, and the opposing tribe leaves.

Horse sports are popular in Panama, and the people enjoy both riding and racing horses. Many Panamanians have ridden in the Kentucky Derby and other major horseraces across the country.

Panama has been successful on the international level in sports. It has produced several champion boxers. Panamanian athletes have prevailed in the Pan-American Games, especially in the sports of weightlifting, track and field, basketball, and swimming. Similar to other Central American athletes, Panamanians have had to overcome political turmoil and financial difficulties to participate in the Pan-American Games. Nevertheless, Panama's athletes have won over 40 medals, including gold ones.

Opposite (top): **A sailing sloop off the coast of Panama.**

Opposite (bottom): **The U.S. influence in Panama extends also to taste in sports.**

A family on a day outing near the Panama Canal.

Most of Panama's casinos are located in Panama City's hotels or at the airport.

URBAN ENTERTAINMENT

Urban Panamanians enjoy the many activities that the cities of Panama, especially Panama City, provide them. Panamanians have many options for leisure activities in Panama City, including shopping, theater, music, nightclubs, and casinos.

SHOPPING Panama City has been called the "Hong Kong of Latin America" because the prices are low and the quantity and quality of goods is high. The main shopping area in the city is along a street called Vía España. Another popular shopping spot is Avenida Central, a street where Panamanians can find many electronic and camera stores along with other types of stores. Panama's best shopping items are cameras, electronic goods, perfume, watches, china, jewelry, mola fabric, leather goods, weavings, and baskets. One difference between shopping in the United States and shopping in Panama is that in Panama, the shopper may bargain with the seller to reach a lower price for the goods.

Because Panama City is a major tourist destination, many of the hotels have shopping centers in them. Panamanians, however, tend to shy away from these areas to avoid the tourists. Like Spain, the shops in Panama close down for lunch and a siesta, or nap, every afternoon. Most shops are open from 8:00 a.m. until noon, and then reopen at 2:00 p.m. to close at 6:00 or 7:00 p.m.

THEATER AND MUSIC Panamanians enjoy attending the theater and musical events during their leisure time. For stage shows, Panamanians prefer the National Theater in the colonial district of Panama City. During the months of February and March, the Folklore Ballet performs at the National Theater. The ballet dancers perform native folk dances in traditional costume. Panama also has movie theaters that show Panamanian and U.S. movies. Although many Panamanians are bilingual, the movies that are in English have Spanish subtitles.

Music is an integral part of most Panamanians' lives. Panamanians particularly enjoy listening to salsa music and other types of rock music. Panama City has the National Symphony for those Panamanians who enjoy classical music, and the city also has many outdoor concerts.

NIGHTLIFE Panamanians enjoy going out at night to restaurants, bars, and casinos. The dance clubs and nightclubs frequently stay open all night so that die-hards can party until dawn.

Panama's government operates its casinos in Panama City. Like Las Vegas in the United States, the casinos attract more tourists than locals. The casinos offer a variety of games to choose from, including roulette, slot machines, poker, blackjack, craps, and jackpot. The Panamanian government does not tax people on the money that they win in gambling.

Relaxing over a game of dominoes.

101

RURAL ENTERTAINMENT

Rural Panamanians enjoy participating in sports and making crafts during their leisure time. Local towns often have baseball and soccer leagues for children and adults. Because many of the rural towns are located in beautiful mountainous regions, local residents enjoy hiking and biking through the countryside.

The Indian tribes that reside in the rural areas of Panama have leisure activities that are gender-based: the men enjoy hunting and fishing, while the women make pottery, arts, crafts, and molas. Many of these activities overlap with the occupations of the tribes.

In the countryside, fairs are a major attraction.

PANAMA'S PRIZE BOXER: ROBERTO DURÁN

Panama's all-time sports hero is the prize boxer, Roberto Durán. This four-time world champion was born in Panama in the early 1950s and grew up on the Panamanian side of the Canal Zone. Durán began his boxing career as an amateur, and when he was 16 years old, the boxing federation chose him to represent Panama in the Pan-American Games. But when the time came for the Panamanian team to leave for the games, they left Durán behind because he would not obey certain rules of politeness. This incident was the country's first glimpse of the volatile and aggressive personality of the man who would become a hero to millions.

Durán turned professional in March 1968. He won his first world championship title just four years later when he defeated Ken Buchanan in the lightweight division.

Durán held the lightweight title for seven years, and then won the World Boxing Association welterweight title in 1980 when he defeated Sugar Ray Leonard. At that time, he was the only man to defeat Leonard in the professional boxing ring.

When Durán defeated Leonard, Panama erupted in celebration. During the celebrations, one person died of a heart attack, two were hit by bullets, and a hospital treated 144 others for heart problems or injuries sustained in the streets of Panama.

Five months after the first fight, the boxers met again. This time, Leonard was victorious. Three years later Durán earned another world championship title when he defeated Davey Moore, the junior middleweight champion, in the eighth round. With this victory Durán became the first boxer in history to win titles in both the lightweight and junior middleweight divisions.

Despite his success, Durán lost two devastating fights in 1983 and 1984, including a knockout by Thomas Hearns. He became severely depressed and gained over 50 pounds. After an 18-month hiatus, he lost the weight and fought again. When he was 37 years old, he won his fourth title by beating middleweight champion Iran Barkley of the United States. Once again, Panamanians celebrated his victory in the streets.

Duran's perseverance and success have earned him the title of Panama's premier athlete. Despite his often explosive personality, many Panamanians idolize him. He has given his country a national sports hero. He continues to fight in 1995 and has no immediate plans to retire.

People have compared Durán to an animal because of the way he fights. Ironically, Durán had a pet that matched his reputation: a 680-pound lion named Walla. Durán kept Walla in his backyard, much to the dismay of his neighbors who did not appreciate Walla's early morning roars.

The San Blas Islands are a popular holiday destination for locals and tourists alike.

When the Shah of Iran left his country in exile in 1979, he stayed on Contadora for a while. This refugee brought international attention to the otherwise quiet vacation spot.

WEEKEND RETREATS

Urban Panamanians escape the cities to enjoy the tranquility of the countryside and beaches. During the year, Panamanians have 16 holidays when businesses, banks, and government offices are closed. City dwellers often take a few extra days off before or after a holiday, and go to the countryside for a long weekend.

Some of the favorite vacation spots for Panamanians are Taboga and Contadora islands, the San Blas Islands, and the beaches along the Caribbean Sea and the Pacific Ocean. Taboga is off the shore of Panama City, and tourists and locals alike flock to the beautiful beaches on this island for sunbathing and water activities. Contadora also is located in the Gulf of Panama and serves as both a relaxing spot for Panamanians and tourists and an international summit center. Several Latin American leaders have met on this island to discuss common problems in their countries; they have become known as the Contadora Group.

The beaches along the Pacific and Atlantic shores are popular retreats for Panamanians. The country is building many new deluxe hotels and casinos in these areas to attract both foreign and domestic vacationers.

FITNESS

Like many other citizens in the world, Panamanians have become concerned about their health in the past few decades. They have realized that good diet, combined with regular exercise, benefits their health. The cities have responded to the fitness craze and built many recreational facilities. Wealthy Panamanians enjoy tennis and golf in their own country, and skiing in Colombia or South American countries. Some middle-class Panamanians can afford to join country clubs to play golf and tennis, and also leave the country for excellent skiing in nearby countries. The majority of Panamanian citizens, however, do not have the money to enjoy these luxurious sports.

Health clubs in the cities are more affordable for many Panamanians. Like the health clubs in the United States, these centers offer aerobics, weightlifting, and swimming to their members. The clubs are not as elaborate as some of the ones in the United States, but they still provide great fitness opportunities for urban dwellers. Panamanians enjoy aerobics, particularly step aerobics, where participants step up and down on a plastic platform while moving their upper body in different ways. This form of exercise strengthens the heart and lungs. Some city dwellers enjoy boxing for recreation and lifting weights.

Because the South American countries are below the equator, the ski season runs from July to September. Panamanians' favorite ski destinations are Portillo, Chile and Bariloche, Argentina.

COCKFIGHTING: A POPULAR SPORT FOR PANAMANIANS

When urban Panamanians leave the cities, they enjoy watching the rural sport of cockfighting. In this game, trained gamecocks fight each other with their beaks. Additionally, the gamecocks often have sharp spurs attached to their legs, which they use to injure one another. Cockfighting includes either two cocks paired against each other or several cocks fighting in a group. The fight ends when one or more of the gamecocks dies or refuses to fight anymore.

FESTIVALS

FESTIVALS IN PANAMA are colorful, musical, and intriguing events that are an important part of every Panamanian's life. Panamanians celebrate birth, death, and marriage. Because Panama is a Roman Catholic country, many of the festivals celebrate religious events. The most exciting festival in Panama is Carnival, which is celebrated through all of Central and South America during the four days before Ash Wednesday. Other important festivals include religious holidays, processions, and nationally significant holidays such as Independence from Spain and Independence from Colombia.

Panamanians call their festivals *fiestas*, ("fee-AYS-tahs") although not all fiestas are "parties," as the word is loosely translated in the United States. Many of the fiestas, primarily the religious ones, are somber events to honor religious figures. The secular fiestas usually include parades and speeches; the religious ones include worship and colorful entertainment such as parades and dances. The native tribes of Panama have their own festivals that incorporate their religious and secular beliefs and include dancing, music, and occasionally, fighting.

Certain events in a Panamanian's life, such as birth, first communion, marriage, and death, are celebrated with a fiesta.

Opposite: **Pilgrims gather at Portobelo every year to pay tribute to the Black Christ.**

Below: **Celebrating Independence Day.**

In small towns the social chasms between the rich and the poor and the different races dissolve as the nation joins together to celebrate Carnival.

CARNIVAL

The biggest fiesta on the Panamanian calendar is Carnival, a celebration that occurs the four days before Ash Wednesday (which is the Wednesday that starts Lent). Roman Catholics always give up some favorite food or activity for Lent, and Carnival is a time to drink, eat, and party in excess in anticipation of the austerity that follows.

All of the Central and South American countries celebrate Carnival. This four-day jubilee originated when Spanish and West African traditions merged in the New World. The West African slaves took advantage of the four-day Spanish holiday to revel in their brief freedom. They turned this time into an elaborate celebration with costumes and traditional music and dance. Today Carnival is one of the biggest festivals in the world.

Carnival in Panama resembles Mardi Gras in New Orleans. Most of the Carnival celebrations consist of *comparsas* ("cohm-PAHR-sahs"), or groups of people dancing, partying, and playing instruments in the streets. Some of the comparsas wear elaborate and colorful costumes that the wearer

January 1	New Year's Day	November 1	National Anthem Day
January 9	Day of National Mourning	November 2	All Souls' Day
February	Carnival Ash Wednesday	November 3	Independence from Colombia Day
March/April	Good Friday Easter	November 4	Flag Day
May 1	Labor Day	November 10	First Call of Independence Day
August 15	Foundation of Panama City (celebrated in Panama City only)	November 28	Independence from Spain Day
		December 8	Immaculate Conception/ Mother's Day
October 11	Revolution Day (not a national holiday)	December 25	Christmas

Although Carnival is a festive occasion, the revelry usually leads to injury. In 1995, 23 Panamanians died during the four-day celebration from auto accidents, murder, or drowning. Five hundred other Panamanians were treated for knife wounds.

began making months before Carnival began. A favorite costume worn by men includes a papier-mâché mask of several colors, a black vest over a white shirt, black pants with ribbons tied in a criss-cross fashion around the calf, an orange or red sash draped across the torso, and a colorful, full skirt made of strips of fabric resembling a man's tie. Some men, who choose not to wear such an elaborate costume, wear guayabera shirts, comfortable black pants, sandals, and a straw hat.

The women usually wear the pollera de gala or "deluxe" pollera for Carnival, complete with elaborate headpieces and jewelry made of gold and pearls.

During Carnival, young men spray the crowds with water to add to the revelry. In the past few years, several towns had to take special measures to have sufficient water for Carnival. The government forbade the use of river water for Carnival because people contracted cholera, an intestinal disease. The towns have managed to haul clean water from other regions of the country so that Carnival can take place.

The people who take part in a religious procession include those who seek help because of unemployment or sickness and repentant Catholics giving thanks or asking forgiveness.

RELIGIOUS PROCESSIONS

Panamanians have many religious processions in honor of personal events, such as birth or marriage, and in honor of religious holidays.

THE PORTOBELO PROCESSION According to Panamanian legend, a wood carving of the Black Christ from a shipwrecked Spanish galleon washed up onto the shores of Portobelo. The fishermen believed that the statue ended a devastating outbreak of cholera in the town. As a token of gratitude, they promised to hold an annual festival in its honor. The inhabitants of Portobelo and thousands of pilgrims from all over Panama continue to honor the Black Christ on October 21 of every year.

On that day, hundreds of people carry the statue of the Black Christ on a platform. These people spend four hours walking through town: for every three steps that they take forward, they take two steps back. Most of the pilgrims and worshippers wear purple robes similar to the one on the Black Christ. The parade ends at the home of the Black Christ—the 18th-century Cathedral of Jesus Nazareno.

THE TABOGA BOAT PROCESSION On the island of Taboga in the Gulf of Panama, the inhabitants hold a religious procession every July to honor the patron saint of the island. Rather than marching through the streets of the island, the inhabitants place the statue in a boat that circles the island. The island also hosts a boat race on this day to honor the saint.

The Statue of the Black Christ is particularly significant to the Afro-Caribbeans because the Christian Savior shares their skin color.

THE TRIBUTE IN SANTIAGO DE VERAGUAS Another Panamanian legend says that a statue of Jesus Christ miraculously appeared in the small town of Santiago de Veraguas many years ago. When the perplexed inhabitants tried to move the statue to another town, it became so heavy that they could not lift it. Thus Panamanians believed that the statue had divine power, and they pay tribute to it on the first Sunday of Lent every year. On this day, the town has a religious procession that ends at the statue. The people bow before the statue and ask it to grant their wishes in return for promised gifts of money, jewels, and sacrifice.

INDEPENDENCE DAYS

Panama celebrates two different independence days. On November 3, the country celebrates its independence from Colombia in 1903; on November 28, it celebrates its independence from Spain.

Panamanians celebrate their independence days with parades, floral displays, and fireworks. All of the government offices, businesses, and shops close on these days so that the employees may join in the national festivities. Many urban Panamanians gather at Independence Square in Panama City for rallies and speeches on Panama's independence.

When Panama regains control of the canal in 1999 and the United States leaves Panama, the citizens probably will celebrate yet another independence day.

FOOD

THE CHIEF AGRICULTURAL products grown in Panama are rice, corn, beans, and coffee. These products are staples in the Panamanian diet. Panamanians have *arroz* ("ah-ROHS"), or rice, with most of their meals, and almost always for lunch. They either eat the rice plain or add meat and vegetables to it. Panamanians often eat both potatoes and rice at one meal.

Panamanians eat corn, another chief product, in a variety of ways. Tortillas are the most popular use of corn in Panama. To make tortillas, rural women or urban factories grind the corn into a flour that is mixed with water. This paste is then formed into thick pancakes called tortillas. Like many other Latin Americans, Panamanians top their tortillas with cheese, meats, and vegetables to make a variety of dishes. The Panamanian tortilla is thick and fried, unlike the Mexican version.

Above: A wheat plantation.

Opposite: **A Cuna Indian husking coconut, one of the tribe's main sources of income.**

True to its name, Panama has an abundance of fish and seafood. The shrimp and lobster of Panama are superb, as are the marlin, sea bass, and snapper. Both the oceans and the fresh water lakes of Panama provide fish for consumption. Chicken and beef also are popular foods for the Panamanian people. Pork is not a popular food in Panama.

Most Panamanian meals include corn tortillas or rice with meat and vegetables or fruit. Yucca is a commonly served vegetable. Cilantro (also called coriander leaf) often is added to soup and sauces for flavor. Other common vegetables are onions, peppers, corn, and tomatoes. The fruits of Panama are numerous, and include pineapples, coconuts, papaya, avocados, watermelon, and citrus fruits.

KITCHENS

Traditionally, women cooked for the family in Panamanian families. In modern Panama, men now share in the tasks of purchasing, preparing, and cooking the food. In rural areas, the roles are still fairly traditional.

Middle- and upper-class Panamanians rarely visit their kitchens, even if the kitchens are modern and up-to-date. Affluent Panamanians usually have a maid who lives with them and cooks and cleans. The maid prepares the meal and serves it to the family in the formal dining room. The family always eat all their meals together in Panama, even if the older members of the family have guests.

Kitchens in rural homes in Panama often are little more than a stove and a countertop. Over the past few decades, the government has provided running water to most rural communities. Some people, however, still must walk to the community well for clean water. The Guaymí Indians of rural Panama usually have a building separate from their house to prepare meals. Sometimes more than one family will share the cooking facility in a Guaymí community.

In both rural and urban areas of Panama, many homes do not have water heaters and the residents must boil water for bathing, cooking, and washing clothes. In the less modern urban homes, gas operates the water heater. One of the family members or the maid must light the heater every morning so that the family can bathe and cook. In the elite areas and regions occupied by U.S. citizens, homes have electric water heaters.

An expensive meal in Panama costs approximately $30 for two people, excluding alcohol and tip. The average dinner for two costs about $20.

EATING OUT

Panamanians love to eat out, and Panama City's residents have a plethora of restaurants from which to choose. A *restaurante* ("res-tow-RAN-tay") is similar to a restaurant in the United States, a *panadería* ("pan-ah-day-REE-ah") sells take-out bread and rolls, a *pastelería* ("pas-tell-ay-REE-ah") offers pastries, a *bar* is similar to a U.S. bar that serves drinks and appetizers, and a *cantina* ("kan-TEE-nah") is a lower-class drinking establishment that women usually do not frequent.

In addition to restaurants that prepare their native food, Panamanians also may choose from many restaurants serving Japanese, Chinese, Italian, Spanish, or French food. Most of the restaurants are moderately priced, so middle- and upper-class Panamanians can afford to dine out often. According to Panamanian manners, the person who invites another to a restaurant or bar pays the bill. Panamanians tip their servers approximately 15% of the bill.

Baked or fried plantains usually accompany the main course at lunch.

EATING HABITS

Panamanians eat three hearty meals per day: *el desayuno* ("day-sigh-OO-noh," breakfast), *el almuerzo* ("ahl-MWER-soh," lunch), and *la cena* ("SAY-nah," dinner). The typical breakfast fare is thick, deep-fried tortillas with a white cheese; sauteed liver, garlic, and onions; and fresh rolls or bread. In the urban areas, Panamanians sometimes have eggs as well. The common breakfast drink in Panama is coffee.

Unlike their neighbors, Panamanians do not consider lunch to be the main meal. A typical lunch begins with soup, followed by chicken or steak. Panamanians serve their meat with a mixture of cooked rice and red kidney beans or pigeon peas. Salad is eaten with the main course.

The dinner meal usually consists of meat covered with a spicy sauce, rice, and salad. Panamanians love dessert, but it is usually only fruit. Occasionally they indulge in cake, chocolate mousse, pie, or cheesecake. After dinner Panamanians enjoy a cup of coffee, such as espresso.

Daily beverages for Panamanians include water, lemonade, fresh fruit juices, soda, and beer.

116

BEER IN PANAMA

Cerveza ("ser-VAY-sa"), or beer, is one of the chief industrial products of Panama. It is a fermented beverage made from malted barley, corn, or rice. The Babylonians and Egyptians began brewing beer over 6,000 years ago, and the recipe spread to Mediterranean countries such as Greece and Spain. The Spanish colonists probably introduced the process to Panamanians, and today, beer production is a major industry.

The brewing of beer occurs through the processes of malting, mashing, boiling and hopping, fermenting, and finishing. The brewer begins the process with cereal grains, yeast, hops, and water.

The first step in brewing beer is preparing the grain, or malting. The brewer immerses the grain in water for one to four days and piles it on a ventilated floor once it is soft. The soft grains germinate small sprouts, and when the sprouts measure three-fourths the length of the kernel, the brewer dries them in a large oven. After slowly increasing the heat to 180^0F (82.8^0C), the brewer removes the sprouts and stores the grain, which is now called malt. After storing the malt for four to eight weeks, the brewer grinds it. The grinding releases an enzyme that converts starch into sugar during the mashing stage.

The brewer mixes the malt with water and adds cereal, such as corn or rice, during the mashing stage. The brewer heats the mixture, called wort, to 154^0F (68.3^0C) and stirs it. The wort forms a natural filter of solids through which a liquid passes through. The brewer stores the liquid wort in barrels.

During this stage, the brewer adds three-fourths a pound of hops, which are dried flowers from the hop vine, to each barrel of wort. The hops add flavor and prevent the beer from spoiling. The brewer boils the wort and hop mixture for three to four hours.

After boiling and hopping, the brewer adds one pound of yeast to every barrel. The yeast causes alcohol and carbon dioxide to form. The fermenting process takes one to two weeks at 38 to 40^0F (3.4 to 4.5^0C).

During the finishing stage, the brewer collects the carbon dioxide with special equipment. The beer settles and clears, and the brewer ages it in metallic vats for three to six weeks. As the beer settles, the carbon dioxide escapes and causes foam to develop. The brewer removes the foam from the vat with long, wide shovels. After it ages, the brewer prepares the beer for the market by carbonating it, chilling the mixture, and passing it through a filter for packaging.

Panamanians enjoy drinking beer, and their local beer is very good. The three favorites are called Panama, Soberna, and Cristal Balboa. The Coors Brewing Company of the United States began selling its beer to Panama in 1992. Panama also imports beer from Germany and Mexico. Thus, Panamanians have a choice of domestic or imported beer. Another popular domestic drink among Panamanians is rum.

FAVORITE FOODS AND REGIONAL DELICACIES

The different regions in Panama have different types of cuisine, but most Panamanians enjoy eating food from all over their country. The food of all regions of Panama usually is quite spicy.

Fish is a common item in the national diet. The most popular fish in Panama is *corvina* ("kohr-VEE-nah"), or sea bass. The favorite appetizer among Panamanians and other Latin Americans is *ceviche* ("say-VEE-chay"). To prepare ceviche, Panamanians season raw sea bass with small yellow and red peppers and thinly sliced onions. They marinate the mixture overnight in lemon juice and serve it raw. Panamanians also use their favorite fish, sea bass, to make *bolitas de pescado* ("boh-LEE-tahs day pes-CAH-doh"), which are breaded and fried balls of fish. Although the shrimp and lobster are excellent in Panama, most Panamanians save these regional delicacies for special occasions.

Sea turtles provide another source of food for Panamanians. Poor rural families eat the eggs of sea turtles as a source of protein, and urban Panamanians view the eggs as a gourmet food. One turtle will lay as many as 150 eggs, and rural Panamanians collect them and sell them for less than one dollar per egg. Over the past few years, the turtle population has declined, so environmentalists are trying to save the eggs from human consumption.

A favorite meat dish among Panamanians is *ropa vieja* ("ROH-pah bee-AY-hah"). To

As seafood is abundant in Panama, many meals include it in a variety of ways.

prepare this dish, Panamanians shred beef and mix it with green peppers, spices, plantains, and rice. Other favorites are *empanadas* ("em-pan-AH-das"), or fried meat pies, and *lomo relleno* (LOH-moh ray-YAY-noh"), which is steak stuffed with spices and herbs.

Panama is famous for its wonderful soups and stews. The traditional soup, *sancocho* ("san-KOH-choh"), is prepared with chicken, corn, plantains, yucca, coriander leaves, and potatoes. Panamanians also use beef and seafood in their stews. *Guacho* is an everyday stew in Panama. Unlike many other Panamanian stews, guacho is more liquid. It contains a lot of different ingredients and provides a complete, nutritional meal.

Iguana is a traditional source of food for rural Panamanians. Urban dwellers also enjoy the delicious taste of iguana meat. Panamanians use both the iguana meat and eggs in their dishes. Because people were hunting iguanas to near extinction, Panama developed a simple method to hatch and rear three different species of iguana.

The most popular Panamanian dessert is *sopa borracha* ("SOH-pah bohr-RAH-chah"), which is pound cake topped with syrup, rum or brandy, cinnamon, raisins, and cloves. If the chef adds whipped cream to sopa borracha, it is called *sopa de gloria* ("SOH-pah day GLO-ree-ah"). Two delicious Panamanian desserts made from rice are *arroz con cacao* ("ahr-ROHS kohn cah-CAH-oh"), a chocolate rice pudding, and *resbaladera* ("rays-bah-lah-THAY-rah"), which is made from rice, milk, vanilla, sugar, and cinnamon.

The Chocó Indians, who continue to maintain their traditional ways, catch their own food and eat iguanas, tapirs, peccary, monkeys, and crocodiles.

Many Panamanians purchase food from outdoor markets that line the streets of the cities or towns.

TABLE MANNERS AND ETIQUETTE

The father always sits at the head of the table. If the family has guests at a meal, the guest of honor sits at the other end of the table. In middle- and upper-class homes, a maid serves the food. She places platters of food on the table, and the diners help themselves. At a formal dinner, however, she serves each person at the table from the platters. Panamanians signal that they have finished a meal by placing their knife and fork vertically and parallel on their plate.

When Panamanians dine at another person's home, good manners dictate that they should eat everything on their plate. If they really dislike something, however, it is not rude to leave it on the plate. Host families serve alcoholic drinks to their guests before, during, and after a meal.

For most meals, Panamanians dress nicely, even if they do not have guests in attendance. When Panamanians visit another person's home for a meal, they wear nice, formal clothes. The men wear a dark suit with a tie, and the women wear a dress.

BLADES' BLACK BEANS

Rubén Blades decided early in life that he did not like chicken and fish, two of the staples in a Panamanian's diet. After spending years in the kitchen with his grandmother and watching her chop chicken and fish, he became a beef fan. He also loves beans, and his favorite dish is a black bean recipe called Blades' Black Beans. He serves the beans with steak, rice, and fried plantains. The following is the recipe:

1 pound (.45 kg) dried black beans, washed and picked over
6 cups chicken stock
4 tablespoons olive oil
1 cup minced yellow onion
1 plum tomato, chopped
1 cup minced green bell pepper
$^1/_4$ cup chopped cilantro (coriander leaf)
1 tablespoon balsamic vinegar
1 tablespoon sugar
2 teaspoons low-sodium soy sauce
1 teaspoon dried oregano
$^1/_8$ teaspoon lemon-pepper seasoning
1 clove garlic, minced
$^1/_4$ pound (.11 kg) baked ham, cut into small pieces
Salt to taste
Sour cream and cilantro sprigs, for garnish

Soak the beans overnight in cold water and drain the following morning. Place the beans in a large, heavy pot and cover with water. Simmer for four hours and add the chicken stock to cover the beans. While the beans are simmering, heat the oil in a skillet over medium high heat. Sauté the onion and add everything but the ham, salt, and garnishes to the skillet. Simmer and stir the mixture for three minutes.

Add the ham and skillet mixture to the pot of beans. Cover and simmer for two hours. If necessary, add more stock to the pot to cover the beans. Season the beans with salt, if desired, and serve the black beans with sour cream and cilantro sprigs. Serves six to eight people.

A potent drink that originated with the native tribes is called chicha *("CHEE-cha"). Chicha is brewed from corn liquor, and Panamanians of all ethnic backgrounds enjoy this robust beverage.*

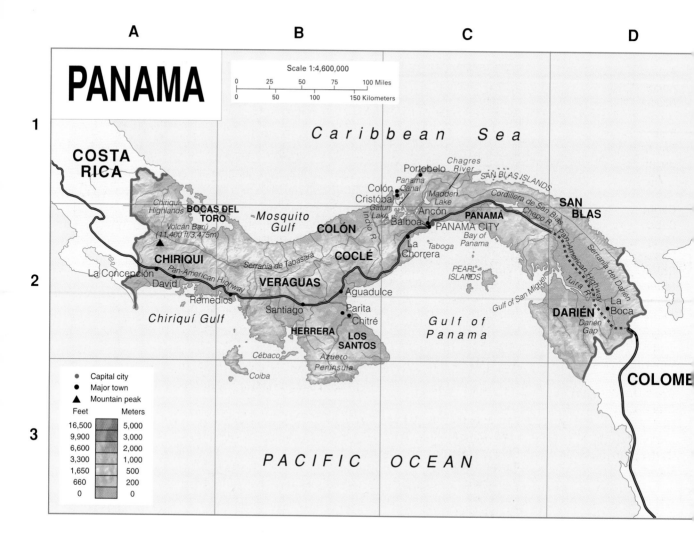

PANAMA

Scale 1:4,600,000

0   25   50   75   100 Miles
0   50   100   150 Kilometers

Caribbean Sea

COSTA RICA

Chiriquí Highlands
BOCAS DEL TORO
Volcán Barú
(11,400 ft/3,475m)

Mosquito Gulf

Portobelo
Chagres River
Panama Canal
Colón
Cristóbal
Madden Lake
Gatún Lake
Indio R.
Ancón
Balboa
SAN BLAS ISLANDS
Cordillera de San Blas
Chepo R.
PANAMÁ
PANAMA CITY
SAN BLAS

CHIRIQUI
COLÓN
La Chorrera
Taboga
Bay of Panama
Pan-American Highway
Serranía del Darién
Tuira R.

La Concepción
David
Pan-American Highway
Serranía de Tabasará
VERAGUAS
COCLÉ
PEARL ISLANDS
La Boca
DARIÉN
Darién Gap

Remedios
Chiriquí Gulf
Santiago
Aguadulce
Parita
Chitré
HERRERA
LOS SANTOS
Gulf of San Miguel
Gulf of Panama

Cébaco
Azuero Peninsula
Coiba

COLOMBIA

● Capital city
● Major town
▲ Mountain peak

Feet	Meters
16,500	5,000
9,900	3,000
6,600	2,000
3,300	1,000
1,650	500
660	200
0	0

PACIFIC OCEAN

QUICK NOTES

OFFICIAL NAME
República de Panamá

AREA
29,762 square miles (77,084 square kilometers)

POPULATION
2.4 million

CAPITAL
Panama City

MAJOR RELIGION
Roman Catholicism

MAJOR RIVERS
Chagres, Chepo, Tuira, Indio

MAJOR LAKE
Gatun

HIGHEST POINT
Volcán Barú (11,400 feet/3,475 m)

CURRENCY
U.S. dollar
Balboa (1 balboa = US$1)

OFFICIAL LANGUAGE
Spanish

FORM OF GOVERNMENT
Republic

TERM FOR CITIZENS
Panamanian(s)

POLITICAL PARTIES
Democratic Revolutionary Party (ruling)
Arnulfista Party
Christian Democrats

LEADERS IN POLITICS
Omar Torrijos
Manuel Noriega
Ernesto Perez Valladares (Current President)

MAIN EXPORTS
Coffee, shrimp, bananas, raw sugar, petroleum products

IMPORTANT ANNIVERSARIES
November 3: Independence from Colombia
November 28: Independence from Spain

NATIONAL ANTHEM
"Himno National de la República de Panamá"

NATIONAL FLOWER
Flower of the Holy Spirit

NATIONAL FLAG
Four rectangles: lower left, blue; lower right, white with centered red star; upper left, white with centered blue star; upper right, red

GLOSSARY

audiencia ("ow-dee-EHN-see-ah")
Spanish court; the basic administrative unit for Spain's American colonies.

chivas ("CHEE-vahs")
Buses with brightly painted panels.

comparsas ("cohm PAHR sahs")
Groups of people celebrating.

cordillera (korh-dee-YAIR-ah")
Mountain chain.

corvina ("kohr-VEE-nah")
Sea bass.

cumbia ("KOOM-byah")
Popular Panamanian dance.

fiesta ("fee-AYS-tah")
Festival or party.

Gross Domestic Product (GDP)
The gross domestic product is the total market value of the goods and services produced by a nation's economy, excluding receipts from overseas. The Gross National Product (GNP) includes receipts from overseas.

gur ("GOOR")
Guaymí ritual for young men.

inna-nega ("een-NAH nay-GAH")
Cuna celebration for young women.

kantule ("kahn-TOO-lay")
Cuna priest.

mejorana ("may-hoh-RAH-na")
Traditional Panamanian folk song.

mestizos ("may-STEE-zos")
Persons of mixed Indian and Spanish or African descent.

mola ("MOH-lah")
Cuna embroidered cloth.

montuno ("mohn-TOO-noh")
National clothing for Panamanian men.

peineta ("peh-ee-NEH-tah")
Headpiece worn with the pollera.

pintado ("pin-TAH-doh")
Straw hat worn by men with the national clothing.

pollera ("poh-YEH-rah")
National dress for Panamanian women: a long, full dress of white cotton with brightly colored embroidery.

salsa
Music that is a blend of rock, jazz, and rhythm and blues with Cuban rhythms.

tamborito ("tahm-moh-REE-toh")
Panamanian national dance.

BIBLIOGRAPHY

Barry, Tom. *Panama: A Country Guide*. Albuquerque: Inter-Hemispheric Education Resource Center, 1990.

Dolan, Edward F. *Panama and the United States: Their Canal, Their Stormy Years*. New York: Franklin Watts, 1990.

Lerner Publications. *Panama—In Pictures*. Minneapolis: Lerner Publications, 1987.

Meditz, Sandra W., and Dennis M. Hanratty, eds. *Panama: A Country Study*. 4th ed. Washington, D.C.: U.S. Government Printing Office, 1989.

St. George, Judith, *Panama Canal: Gateway to the World*. New York: G.P. Putnam, 1989.

Stewart, Gail. *Panama*. New York: Crestwood House, 1990.

Vázquez, Ana Maria B. *Enchantment of the World: Panama*. Chicago: Children's Press, 1991.

INDEX

INDEX

INDEX

Picture Credits

Andes Press Agency: 3, 5, 32, 36, 46, 61, 67, 72, 75, 76, 81, 82, 91, 100, 102, 107, 118
Camera Press: 21, 23, 24, 25, 26, 35, 47, 48, 63, 98, 101
DDB Stock Photo: 13, 31, 34, 38, 44, 58, 60, 65, 69, 86, 87, 88, 97, 104, 114, 120
Embassy of Panama: 15, 27
Image Bank: 17, 96, 113, 123
Impact Photos: 14
Hulton Deutsch: 18, 20, 22
Hutchison Library: 3, 6, 7, 8, 11, 12, 19, 29, 41, 42, 52, 53, 54, 56, 59, 70, 89, 94, 95, 112, 119
Danny Lehman: cover, 4, 10, 33, 39, 45, 50, 51, 62, 66, 71, 78, 84, 90, 106, 108, 110, 116
C. and R. Peterson: 16, 79, 83
Reuters Visnews Library: 30
David Simson: 55, 98
South American Pictures: 28, 37, 43, 57, 68, 92, 93